ONCE A CAMERON HIGHLANDER

First edition, published in 2000 by

WOODFIELD PUBLISHING
Woodfield House, Babsham Lane, Bognor Regis
West Sussex PO21 5EL, England.

ISBN 1-873203-83-7

Once a Cameron Highlander

ROBERT BURNS

Woodfield Publishing
BOGNOR REGIS · SUSSEX · ENGLAND

Frontispiece

The front cover illustration is a detail from a painting *Seventh Camerons on Hill 70 – 25 September 1915* by Joseph Gray. The original painting hangs in the regimental museum at Fort George, Inverness. Permission to use it was kindly granted by Lt-Col A.A. Fairrie, curator.

> "Lieutenant-Colonel Sandilands of the 7th Camerons arrived on the hill. Being the senior officer present, he took command and planted the Headquarters flag of his Battalion on the top. It was his business to recall the van of the advance, now lost in the fog and smoke of the eastern slopes, and to entrench himself on the summit. The Redoubt was now out of our hands, and the line taken ran just under the crest on the west, and was continued North of Loos by the 46th Brigade. To retire the van was no light task. Two officers whose names deserve to be remembered, Major Chrichton of the 10th Gordons, and Major Barron of the 7th Camerons, volunteered for the desperate mission. They fell in the task, but the order reached the stragglers, and they began to fight their way back. In the midst of encircling fire it was a forlorn hope, and few returned to the British lines on the hill. All down the slopes towards Loos lay the tartans Gordon and Black Watch, Seaforth and Cameron, like the drift left on the shore when the tide has ebbed."
>
> John Buchan in *Nelson's History of the War.*

Robert Burns, pictured at Glebelands in 1996,
on the occasion of his 100th birthday.

Foreword

This is the diary, not of a general, or even of a much decorated commander. On the contrary, it is the diary of ordinary private soldier of the First World War — if any of that heroic generation can be described as 'ordinary'.

It details the enthusiasms, the joys, the horrors and the pain of a young man who, at the age of just 18, volunteered with his school-friends to join the army within weeks of the outbreak of war. Despite their fond belief that they would be 'home by Christmas', they soon found themselves caught up in the greatest war in history – their lives swept along on a tidal wave of irresistible force from which none could find shelter.

I count myself privileged to have come to know Robert Burns. Fiercely proud of having served in the 7th battalion of the Queen's Own Cameron Highlanders, known as the 'Shiny Seventh', he was one of the fortunate ones who came through the Battle of the Somme and other battles of the 1914/18 war and made it home. Amazingly born in the 19th-century, he has survived to see the 21st. As I write this forward he is within one month celebrating his 105th birthday and, as important, remains in possession of all his faculties. I salute him and all his gallant comrades, for it is thanks to their courage and sacrifice that we live in peace and liberty today.

Winston S. Churchill

5th October 2000

Introduction

Although the matter contained in this book covers practically the whole period of the First World War, it is neither intended to be a history of that war, nor of the part played by the 79th Regiment of Foot Queens Own Cameron Highlanders.

It is simply a record of my personal experiences from 1914 to 1919, during which time I served with the 7th Battalion, attached to the 44th Highland Brigade of the 15th Scottish Division and also with the 3rd Battalion of that famous Regiment, which was – and still is – the pride of Inverness-shire.

My attachment to Brigade Headquarters gave me the opportunity of becoming knowledgeable of certain details, some of which are included in this book.

Robert Burns 2000

Robert celebrating his 101st birthday on 12th November 1996 with the Queen and Prince Philip at the Royal premiere of the film 'True Blue'. During the evening he was taken on stage and all the audience sang 'Happy Birthday'.

Publisher's Note

When Robert Burns' great-niece, Gaye Huxley, first asked me if I would be interested in publishing *Once Cameron Highlander*, I was amazed to learn that he was 104 years old and was something of a celebrity, being the last surviving member of the Cameron Highlanders to have fought in World War I. Quite remarkably, despite his age, he was still fulfilling dozens of social engagements every year, and was constantly in demand by the press and TV and as a guest of honour at numerous social functions from film premieres to commemorative services, where he mingled with celebrities and royalty and was clearly greatly admired and respected by all.

I immediately agreed to publish this book, based on Robert's First World War diary. It is very matter-of-fact and does not seek to sensationalise his wartime experiences. Nevertheless, it contains many disturbing passages that will give modern-day readers an insight into the horrors that he and his comrades faced on a daily basis in the trenches – particularly at major engagements such as the Battle of Loos in 1915 and the Battle of the Somme in 1916. Robert considered himself 'lucky' to have sustained an injury during the Battle of the Somme serious enough to render him unfit for further fighting in the trenches. More than 1,100 of his fellow Cameron's were not so fortunate and died on the battlefields in France. Robert never forgot them. Every Armistice Day he was to be found proudly standing on parade at the Cenotaph in Whitehall to salute his fallen comrades. He also made pilgrimages to France, gave interviews to Press and TV, spoke to schoolchildren and made every effort to ensure that the valiant fighting spirit of his fellow Scots would never be forgotten.

It was originally our intention to publish this book in time for Robert's 105th birthday on 12th November 2000, but sadly Robert died on the 29th October 2000. It is a matter of great regret to me that I never had the opportunity to meet him in person. I know that his family and many friends will miss him greatly, and I hope that this book will be regarded as a fitting tribute to such a remarkable man. Those who, like me, were not fortunate enough to know Robert personally, will be amazed to discover the story of his life and times recorded here.

Bob Burns – Robert's son – has asked that all royalties from the sale of this book be donated to the Cinemato-graph and Television Benevolent Fund (CTBF) who looked after Robert so splendidly in his final years.

Nick Shepperd
Publisher

Contents

APPENDICES

CHAPTER 1 – [1914]

The King's Shilling

The tap-tap of my typewriter, in rhythm with the left-right left-right of the new recruits marching down Buchanan Street headed by a robust piper, came to an abrupt end when the office manager arrived unexpectedly.

As I looked down from the vantage point my first floor balcony window – a daily occurrence – I was longing to be part of that chorus-singing human crocodile, half of it in step and the other half not – with the lone piper up ahead, carrying on regardless.

This 'bowler-hat brigade', as it was known, was enthusiastically cheered by onlookers from office windows on each side of the street, and as the days passed, bowler hats were gradually replaced by 'skips' (which cost only one shilling and sixpence) until they were all sold out.

Inculcated with patriotic fervour and having an innate craving for adventure, I needed no prompting to ask to be relieved of my sedentary shorthand-typist/cashier job in an insurance office.

Every morning for weeks, as I left my country home, I was waved 'au revoir' by the twenty or so Walloons who had been thrust upon us in our 'boarding establishment' as it was then called.

They had been forced to flee their homes in Belgium and had brought nothing with them except memories of their families. As they told me their stories I felt that I ought to impress upon them that we Scots were all eager to do something to help them get back to their homes.

My pal Jimmy was very touched when I related what they had been through and became as keen as I to spend a holiday with these unfortunates when they had returned to Belgium after the war. I was particularly keen to do this, as I had already visited their country.

And so, together, Jimmy and I went to a recruiting office, where after only a few minutes the sergeant recommended me to "gang back ter me mither" as I was too young (by a matter of days!).

What a disappointment.

Undaunted and not to be outdone, we found a second recruiting office in another part of Glasgow where, having lied about my exact age, I was duly accepted. This bold step took place on the 6th November 1914.

As a volunteer, I had the option of choosing which regiment I wished to join. Ever since the war started, I had decided that if I were to enlist, my first choice would be the Cameron Highlanders.

Why the Camerons?

Because of their kilts.

When only an infant, I wore a kilt most of the time, and continued to do so until leaving the village school when I was twelve. We lived in Johnston, when I was about six years old, I remember a Hansom-cab, with the driver perched high up at the back, calling to take me, my brother and my sister to 'dance classes'.

The professor who taught us, an old man with white moustache and scratchy fiddle, apparently complained to my parents about the 'nasty habit' we boys had of putting our hands in our trouser pockets. Thereafter, to appease the professor, my brother and I had to attend the classes dressed in kilts.

Because my mother was a 'Gordon', my brother had been christened 'Gordon' and had the honour of wearing the Gordon tartan. I, to be different, wore the Cameron tartan. And it was the Cameron tartan that I wore throughout my childhood until I left the village school to travel to Glasgow – hence my longing to become a member of the Cameron Clan.

After Jimmy and I had decided which regiment we wished to join, everything seemed to be in order and the sergeant handed each of us the 'King's Shilling'.

We thereupon took the shortest route to Lockhart's Tea Rooms where we celebrated – and still had a few coppers left afterwards!

When I returned home to break the news to my family, no one seemed the least surprised, although there was a little excitement.

Before long the whole village was aware that I had 'jined the sogers', and indeed, I was the first villager to do so. As a consequence, the Minister, the Rev, James Buchanan DD, popped over to see me, as did the Headmaster, James Browning MA, who was very interested as his only son Arthur was about to apply for a commission in the Glasgow Highlanders.

However, the younger element in my away-from-it-all village lacked any interest or enthusiasm. One was heard to say sarcastically "Whit a fine soger *he'll* make!"

I admit that compared to the hardy pre-war regular soldiers I must have seemed a weakling in his eyes.

CHAPTER 2 – [1914]

Inverness

After the outbreak of war on the 4th August, it was widely predicted that it would be 'all over in six months' – hence by ambition to 'get in' before it was too late and I missed all the excitement.

Only three days after enlisting, I entrained at Buchanan Street for Inverness, the capital of the Highlands, accompanied by many more new recruits and some 'old soldiers' returning from 'draft leave'.

It was an interesting journey through snow-covered countryside with which I was unfamiliar. I spent most of my time in the corridor and was intrigued by the antics of the Highland deer as the two-engine train puff-puffed its leisurely way up the mountain slopes. The deer lined up at the track-side, evidently expecting to be given titbits in accordance with custom, whilst in the background roamed enormous Highland cattle with huge horns.

A hefty, kilted NCO was told 'yes' when he asked me if I was going up to join the Camerons.

"Ah, well, m'lad, don't forget that once a Cameron always a Gentleman". (The actual motto was 'Once a Cameron always a Cameron).

I asked him what difference that made to me and he said "You'll be neither a Cameron nor a Gentleman until you get your hair cut!"

Fearful of what the battalion barber might do to us, we rookies adopted his suggestion and went to a barber's shop near the station before doing anything else and had a 'very short back and sides'. From what we saw later, this proved to be wise!

On the train was another old soldier who seemed more than friendly, but when wishing me luck he asked me if I had any money. I must have looked suspicious, but he soon put me at my ease when he said "When yee get oot o' the station there's a wee shop jist opposite that sells money belts. Buy yin o' then an' keep your money roon yer waist – even when yer sleepin'". A very sensible idea, and to my surprise it was rare to come across anyone who was *not* wearing a money belt.

From the centre of town it was about a mile to the barracks – but what a climb from the main road! However we had no difficulty in locating where we were to report. Without much palaver I was given a number – S/14141 Private.

My next move was to the Quartermaster's Stores where I was measured up and handed an assortment of clothing a holdall for darning and sewing plus a Krupp razor – yes Krupp, the same firm that was manufacturing the guns to kill us!

Next in importance was bedding. Very simple.

"Take this down to the stables and fill it with straw."

The linen paillasse was about six feet long, thirty inches wide at the top and twelve inches at the foot. Somewhat menacingly, it resembled the shape of a coffin when stuffed with straw, dead thistles, dandelions or any other weeds that could be found, but looked quite respectable once enshrouded in blankets, provided it had been filled with some care.

What a first night that was! Sleeping on the floor was strange enough. In the morning there was Jimmy on his hands and knees looking for his 'dummies' (fancy having false teeth at only 19 years of age! Fortunately he found them.)

"Ha-Ha, no shave."

"He-he, no razor," was a very common exchange.

On an inspection parade several were 'up for it' for not having shaved – including myself.

Although I had reached an age where I thought it was still not necessary to shave, I was told to "get on with it and report back to the Guard Room at 7pm". A dirty trick, for that was the hour we would normally be going off to amuse ourselves in town.

So, with my new Krupp (open) razor I obeyed orders. Most of the baby chins were OK but when three of us reported as instructed, the sergeant, no doubt thinking he was adding a touch of humour, said he couldn't recognise us and told us to go and 'clean our bloody faces'.

At the bottom of the steep steps (probably about a hundred) leading from the parade ground was the Milburn Distillery. Part of it was taken over so as to accommodate the ever-increasing number of recruits. Why I was transferred there beats me, but to make the best of the circumstances there was only one solution; brush the hops or whatever they were off the floor and persevere in getting them to stay piled up against the wall. Some men found it more comfortable to sleep *on* the hops in preference to a concrete floor with only two blankets and no paillasse.

For ablution purposes there was a granite horse-trough in the open snow-covered yard, the early risers having the unenviable task of breaking the ice. Those who had to shave got over the handicap by putting some cold water in an empty Woodbine tin and heating it over a candle. As often as not, more than one shaving brush would find its way into the tin!

We went to a church service in the town. In comparison with the modest church in our little village, St Andrew's Cathedral was a magnificent edifice. There was lively music, and my buddy and I thought it must be coming from a band playing outside. We were both mistaken; it was the church organ, which we could not see, that was responsible for the sound. Such a volume of the music could never have been produced by the bellows-type contraption we had in our little church at home. It certainly was an experience to be part of such a large congregation with almost everyone in some sort of uniform.

I shall always remember part of the Sermon:

> *"...and every time you dishonour a girl,*
> *you put a nail in her coffin."*

Having left school at the early age of fourteen I was innocently ignorant as to what was implied. It was only after barrack-room discussion with an old soldier who had heard the story before, that we understood!

The reception and wonderful kindness bestowed upon us by the people of Inverness will not be forgotten so long as there are Cameron Highlanders.

I recall going into a 'Welcome Centre' one night, my coat absolutely drenched. I was invited to take it off so that it could be partially dried while I was enjoying my tea and cakes, for which no charge was made. When I intimated that it was time to return to the barracks, instead of being given my coat, I was handed a different one (civilian type, like my own) and asked to return it to the gentleman next time I was in town, when I would find my own coat nice and dry. That gentleman's name was 'Davidson' of Davidson & Sons, family butchers in Queen Street.

With the arrival of new recruits every day, it was no surprise to learn that to provide accommodation for them we would shortly be on the move.

We were now over 1,100 strong and had been formed into the 7th Battalion Queen's Own Cameron Highlanders – the 79th Regiment of Foot. I was in "D" company of the 16th Platoon – the rearmost platoon in an infantry regiment when in marching order, and therefore, about the last man in the battalion – except of course when it was 'about turn'.

Looking and feeling like real soldiers, our adventures were about to begin and on a memorable day too – St Andrew's Day, 30th November 1914.

Jauntily, we marched off towards the railway station. The nearer to the centre of the town we got, the louder the cheers from the people lining the street became – except for those with tear-laden eyes.

News of our imminent departure must have been no secret, as evidenced by the distribution by onlookers of so many food parcels, cigarettes and knitted comforts. Despite the huge number of spectators looking for their 'favourites' I was fortunate that a friend picked me out to give me a parcel.

We considered ourselves unlucky in not being able to remain in Inverness to celebrate Christmas and New Year with these people who had been like fathers and mothers to us. When men returned to their barracks at night it was always interesting to listen to their stories of the wonderful times they had, mostly in private homes.

When celebrating our *last* night our conversation switched back to our *first* night in the Army. After making up our beds, Jimmy and I went into town. On our return we found that our beds had been taken! It appeared that a batch of new recruits from a mining area had arrived on a late train and had promptly commandeered our beds and taken them to another Quarter. As it was after 'Lights Out' we had to make do with just two blankets and rough it on the floor. A hard life, that of a soldier.

CHAPTER 3 – [1914]

Aldershot

Some twenty hours after puff-puffing out of the station we arrived at Aldershot without a welcome. What a contrast to the vociferous cheers and 'farewells' when we left that beautiful town of Inverness.

Once aboard the train it did not take much time to devour the minute pack of army rations handed to us on departure, so the many gift parcels thrust upon us on our march to the station were greatly appreciated.

What an uncomfortable journey we endured through the night in a cold compartment with scarcely room to move. The only diversion apart from trying to snooze was playing 'banker' – which was to be the downfall of the young and inexperienced, including myself.

Our first impression of Salamanca Barracks was that they resembled prison buildings of the type one saw in films. Inside, our quarters were long and narrow with no daylight except through the door and at the extreme end. One of the regulars sharing our room told us that there were twice as many men in the barracks as was the case in peacetime: we were really crammed in.

When we arrived, the swift-of-foot claimed an iron bedstead whereas the others (the well-brought up ones) had to be content with a place on the floor. In fact, many beds had been removed in order to provide more accommodation on the floor, which was wooden, thank goodness.

We wondered what was happening when in came about a dozen really robust, tall and unshaven 'foreign speaking' individuals. They had just arrived from the Outer Hebrides and not one of them could understand even the simplest of orders. Every night just before 'Lights Out' they would gather in a corner, squat on the floor and join in with prayers that the rest of us could not understand. Soon, with a Gaelic-speaking sergeant, they just vanished – probably transferred to a non-combatant unit.

Barrack-room life was anything but miserable and the sprinkling of 'old soldiers' made it very clear that we should adjust our ways to our new life as quickly as possible, and forget what or who we were in civvy street – rich, poor, educated or ignorant.

After canteen hours, when everyone was back in quarters to answer 'roll-call' was when real camaraderie became evident and when we all became 'tarred with the same brush'.

We learned a few 'for-soldiers-ears-only' songs. One rookie, having managed to find his way back from the canteen, insisted on inflicting upon us what he called "the best song in the world" which – according to Lowland rendition – went something like this:

"Oh Tallietoodalum, nae mater whaur ye be
Tallietoodalum Cas'le will aye be dear tae me
A wid'na seen ma Mary had a no gaun tae see
Tallietoodalum Cas'le an' its bonnie scenery."

I do not know how many verses there were, but the song remained very popular in our company, particularly after canteen hours.

For those who did not see eye-to-eye with the King's Regulations there was always suitable accommodation available in the much-dreaded 'Glasshouse' which I never did actually see, being wise enough to keep out of trouble. Besides, in view of the stories I had heard, I was scared stiff of doing anything wrong.

I recall on one occasion being 'nosey-parkerish' and making my way to a special 'show' that was taking place at a canteen. I was advised by an Old Soldier to keep away as I was "much too young for beer and dancing women"!

I will say that a few Old Soldiers – too old for active service – were very understanding and at Christmas time really looked after us, particularly the Army cooks.

Most of us youngsters had soft drinks as we dared not run the risk of taking anything stronger in case we finished up 'in the clink'.

A Piper playing 'Reveille' at 6am and a bugle sounding 'Fall In' at 6.30am was bad enough, but fancy having to run two miles or so on a cold morning without breakfast. After a few mornings of this routine, with several falling out and others being ill on their return, the Medical Officer, I learned, insisted that in future we must not exercise on an empty stomach. So it came to pass that we had a bowl of tea before setting out on subsequent runs.

One good point about Salamanca Barracks was that they were situated quite near to the town. Apart from the Sausage 'n' Mash shops (we had plenty of these in the barracks) there were many other places where we could meet, eat and enjoy a change of company, although never oblivious to the fact that we were compelled to restrict our convivialities to keep within what we could afford on our one-shilling-a-day soldier's pay.

A KILT! At last I managed to borrow one. I was one of the lucky ones. I rushed down into Aldershot to be photographed and wasted no time in sending copies back home. The delay in issuing kilts was due to the necessity of sending replacements overseas. Further uneasiness was caused by rumours that we were not to have tartan kilts on account of the expense. Khaki ones were proposed but I believe the Scottish 'higher-ups' protested at such a suggestion, as each Clan had for hundreds of years been proud of its tartan.

Barrack life all too soon became anything but cheerful; too much 'rule-of-thumb' and 'do-it-by-numbers' for we poor amateurs, and the lack of comfort and very poor mess facilities were not what we expected to find in permanent peacetime quarters. The one consolation was that we were scheduled to be here for only a short time – and that, indeed, turned out to be the case.

CHAPTER 4 – [1915]

Kitchener

Happily, our six-week sojourn at Aldershot was over on the 15th January 1915, then off we cheerfully marched to Liphook, Hampshire.

So far as billets were concerned I was lucky, I was conducted to "Oudtshoorn" Portsmouth Road and was well-received by a rather nice family. What a contrast from those prison-like barracks at Aldershot!

How can I forget the 22nd February 1915? The battalion started off on what was thought as just an ordinary routine march. The rank and file therefore were unaware of the importance of the occasion – inspection by a French General and Lord Kitchener. Yes, the real Kitchener, not the one on the hoardings declaring "Your Country Needs You" with his finger pointing at you no matter what angle you looked at him.

It had been snowing throughout the previous night and early morning. After struggling umpteen miles through near-blizzard conditions, we halted on Frensham

Common. It took a considerable amount of shuffling from right to left, backwards and forwards and vice versa before we eventually attained inspection formation. Thus the 7th Cameron Highlanders became an integral part of the 15th Scottish Division. What a sight it was to see so many thousands of soldiers spread out on that Heath!

Some of the soldiers were certainly more comfortably clad that we poor 'kilties' who were still unaccustomed to exposing their knees even under normal weather conditions.

"Attention!" – False alarm.

"Stand at ease!"

And this we were only too glad to do.

For three hours we stood on that snow-covered common, stamping feet or swinging arms in an endeavour to keep warm, with the wind and sleet adding to our discomfort . Some men collapsed either due to fatigue, hunger or sheer cold, and as there were no stretcher bearers or Royal Army Medical Corps (RAMC) to be seen, the 'casualties' were discreetly carried off 'behind the scenes'.

At last there was a stir, and we were called once more to 'Attention'. Along the road came the 'Brass', seated on prancing horses. Behind them and about a hundred yards from where we were lined up, Lord Kitchener and his party, in cars, approached slowly and without stopping to carry out a close inspection of we Camerons, passed out of sight.

No doubt the men in the front ranks of the various units on either side of the road came under his eye, but we were disappointed. It was an agonising day on Frensham Common, but one that made us realise that as soldiers we had to carry on whatever the hardships or circumstances. This unexpected exposure in the snow reminded me of pictures I had seen in my school-days of 'Napoleon's Retreat from Moscow'.

On the 25th February we moved to Cirencester. I was allocated a room in the Five Bells (or was it Eight Bells). Not being a drinker I told the sergeant I did not want to sleep in a pub and asked for somewhere different. He told me to find somewhere else (if I could) and report back to him as soon as possible.

I popped into a baker's shop where the owner Mrs Viner agreed to take me in and before long I was tucking into tea and cakes. What luck! I was just on the point of going back to tell the sergeant that I managed to get fixed up when who should walk in but himself, he had not yet found a place.

So far as I was concerned everything in the garden was lovely, for it was springtime and I was quite happy in this lovely little town. We underwent rather more strenuous training than hitherto but as this took place out in the open country it was tolerable when compared to barrack square routine.

However fatigued one was after a hard day's work, there was always the consolation of having a comfortable home to go back to. The social side of soldiering was all that could be wished for and after six weeks, during which we became part of this small town, many friendships were formed. I know of one man who actually married a girl he met at a dance. When we finally left, there were many heartbreaks and as can be imagined many men returned there when they were granted weekend leave.

CHAPTER 5 – [1915]

Salisbury Plain

On the 6th April we proceeded to Chiseldon Camp on Salisbury Plain. There we were accommodated in recently constructed hutments – so new that we could smell the timber. The NCO in charge of each hut was lucky as he had a little room to himself near the entrance. Midway along was a stand up stove, away from the wall with a narrow chimney. When lit at night it was dangerously red-hot – particularly the chimney as it protruded through the wooden roof. Huts, huts, huts everywhere and not a tree in view! Isolated from civilians and nothing to dispel homesickness there was ample time to write to the many friends who had been so kind to us in Cirencester where we were really spoilt. There was never any need to ask anyone where he was going for the weekend.

In addition to the regular 'spit and polish' we were obliged to carry out innumerable 'fatigues' – such as cleaning the floor, scrubbing tables and seats and doing windows more often than was necessary.

Everything was now being done 'at the double', giving the impression that we were preparing to jump off at any minute.

My pal Jimmy was a battalion scout and being attached to the Orderly Room was conversant with the various programmes. Rifle practice was the next important item on the list, and under his breath he told me that those who failed the test would have to return to the ranges on the following day for further instruction and practice.

Furnished with this information I made sure that all my efforts to strike the bull were futile. I was a complete failure initially and therefore listed to go back to the ranges the following day. My second session was a great success! And whilst I and a few others were undergoing the second test, the remainder of the battalion was slogging along on a twenty-five mile route march with full pack!

We who were at the ranges were back at the camp in time to cheer up those who had been trudging it for many hours over an uninteresting plain. As a recompense for their exertions, the next day was regarded as a rest day. And so it was – lots of football – proving that the men were in good shape, physically.

At the end of April, Colonel Haig left us and command of the battalion was taken over by Colonel Sandilands, DSO who had been with the 46th Brigade. I shall always remember him by his small, heavy but tidy 'sandy' moustache and by his soft-upper riding boots which matched his moustache in colour. He was a striking personality, and even more so when mounted on horseback.

We were right in guessing that a move was contemplated for on the 12th May 1915 we hoofed it to Parkhouse Camp which was situated on a different part of the Plain. It was in this camp that the real hardening-up process began, and the longer it lasted the more intensified became our desire to get away from mock battles and to participate in the real thing – 'over there'.

15th May 1915 – another full-kit route march. This turned out to be a march-past by the whole Brigade as Kitchener and his aides de camp looked on.

On the 25th May we set out on manoeuvres which lasted two days and one night. It certainly was no picnic – one reason being that there was a shortage of food. Whilst lying on the ground 'hiding' from the 'enemy' I prized open a tin of condensed milk with my bayonet and two of us gluttonously disposed of it, but with a sickening after effect.

After lying out all night in the dampness it was a relief when we wearily wandered back and I was glad to flop down on my trestle-bed in Hut No. 7, lucky once again for some men had to 'doss out' in tents as there were as yet insufficient huts.

An essential part of our equipment was a small bag of 'iron rations' which had to be kept in our haversacks. To be precise, these rations were tiny iron-hard biscuits which were not to be eaten except in an emergency and then only with permission.

There was one occasion when I and a dozen more, to avoid starvation, innocently ate our biscuits. My water bottle was empty and despite the risk of being sick again fell back on condensed milk to help the fodder away. Little did we then realise the severity of the punishment that could have been meted out for this infringement.

On 'kit inspection' when it was found that the iron rations had been eaten without permission, the guilty were 'confined to barracks' for twenty-four hours – this regardless of a plea that we had not been instructed as to when or when not they may be eaten.

If there was anything I disliked it was having to do guard duty. This entailed being on alert at the entrance to the camp, or guard room, from 6pm until the same time next day.

Apart from the "Halt who goes there?" routine the officer-of-the-day could come along at any old time, day or night, and ask the sentry to call out the Guard and if it did not come out promptly with each man properly dressed, trouble was bound to ensue.

To uphold the tradition of the Shiny Seventh (us) someone 'high up' had a brilliant idea: nominate an extra man for guard duty. Bearing in mind that 'a good soldier is always on parade five minutes early' I took great care that I was never late.

When all had reported at the Guard Room, the Orderly Officer would carry out a minute inspection (including looking down the barrel of each man's rifle) and then decided which man was the cleanest, smartest and the most soldier-like. Then it was "step forward Private so-and-so. Dismiss!" The "so and so", exempt from Guard Duty would 'right turn' salute and march away briskly. I made a point of ensuring that my rifle, buttons, badge, heels of my boots – and even the instep of the soles – were impeccably clean and shiny as far as possible. Once more my luck was in – I am 'best man' – so no sitting up all night for me!

Parkhouse Camp, in its isolated position on Salisbury Plain, sorely lacked social activities. The possibility of an early departure overseas was foremost in the minds of everyone but despite the surreptitious quizzing from day to day we were no nearer to learning the secret as to 'when'.

There was something unusual happening not far away. It was an open-air Riding School for Officers. To me, a 'horsy' chap from childhood, it was really amusing to see junior subalterns and others bobbing up and down uncomfortably, thrown off by their mounts, and often lacking the experience to remount unaided. All this time the riding master (from a yeoman unit no doubt) was yelling at the top of his voice (as was his prerogative).

"You there ... what the **** are you playing at?

It must have been rather embarrassing, to say the least, for a young officer to be put through the mill like this in front of a laughing audience from the lower ranks of his own unit. Unfortunately for us, however, the free entertainment came to an abrupt end when we were ordered away from the ring.

On the 3rd June our all-kilted Brigade held a 'Highland Games' – and the Camerons gained more points than the other three regiments and had the honour of being presented with a Silver Bugle by Brigadier General Wilkins.

The 21st June was another outstanding day – just as we anticipated it would be – because of the extra spit and polish demanded of us in addition to other abnormal activities taking place throughout the camp. It all culminated in the Division being inspected by the King.

4th July 1915 – today it was made known that we were to prepare to go OVERSEAS, which meant that all superfluous kit had to be disposed of without delay. Then came the search for brown paper and string to parcel up the personal items to be sent home. It was a welcome confirmation of the good news when each on of us was handed a copy of Lord Kitchener's message which read:

(This paper is to be considered by each Soldier as Confidential and to be kept in his Active Service Pay Book)

You are ordered abroad as a soldier of The King to help our French comrades against the invasion of a common enemy. You will have to perform a task which will need your courage, your energy, your patience. Remember that the honour of the British Army depends on your individual conduct.

It will be your duty not only to set an example of discipline and perfect steadiness under fire but also to maintain the most friendly relations with those with whom you are helping in this struggle.

The operations in which you are engaged will, for the most part, take place in a friendly country, and you can do your own country no better service than in showing yourself in France and Belgium in the true character of a British soldier. Be invariably courteous, considerate and kind.

Never do anything likely to injure or destroy property and always look upon looting as a disgraceful act.

You are sure to meet with a welcome and be trusted: your conduct must justify that welcome and that trust.

Your duty cannot be done unless your health is sound. So keep constantly on your guard against any excesses.

In this new experience you may find temptation both in wine and women. You must entirely resist both temptations and while treating all women with perfect courtesy, you should avoid intimacy.

> *Do your duty bravely*
> *Fear God*
> *Honour the King*
>
> *KITCHENER*
> *Field-Marshal*

Overseas

Now we know what was in store for us. The 44th Highland Brigade has been formed and is made up as follows:

7th Battalion – Queen's Own Cameron Highlanders
8th Battalion – Seaforth Highlanders
9th Battalion – Black Watch
10th Battalion – Gordon Highlanders

We are the only all-kilted Brigade in the Army, at the present time and is included in the 15th Scottish Division.

We swung out of Parkhouse Camp and cheerfully slogged it to Tidworth Station where there were thousands of troops, field kitchens etc. With ten in a carriage, plus equipment, we were chugged out of the station at 6.30pm.

This was the moment we had been waiting for. When would we be back? Most of us were of the opinion that it would all be over in six months! And that was probably one of the reasons why so many rushed to volunteer. So it was on the night of the 8th July 1915 that we embarked on the SS *Arundel* at Folkestone.

Scarcely had I got the loaded pack off my back when I was given a job. Accompanied by a sergeant, stepping or stumbling over cables, ropes etc, I made my way to the 'sharp end' of the ship.

I was instructed by the sergeant to look out for anything that seemed untoward during the crossing, and if I saw anything, I was to ring the bell and remain at my post until he or someone else came along. (In my opinion this responsible duty should have been delegated to someone of higher rank than a Private). However, as we nosed our way through a choppy sea and about half-an-hour after our departure, I saw a little light down in the darkness.

A submarine? Oh no, surely not! Nevertheless, I gave that bell a rough time until someone came hurriedly towards me – more excited than I was. There was intense activity before it was revealed that the light I had seen was that of the pilot boat returning to Port! Despite the hubbub, accompanied by some real military language, it was agreed that I had been justified in ringing the alarm on this occasion.

It was now time for me to be relieved, and I was more than happy to get away from the incessant dipping and swaying and the consequent drenching by a windswept salty spray.

The lights of Boulogne Harbour were now faintly penetrating the darkness. The ship, although not now in the open channel, was still bobbing up and down much to my personal discomfort. I couldn't 'hold it' any longer and just had to 'bring it up' – amidst laughter and no sympathy.

I sat down on the deck, really ill, wet and shivering. Not for long however, as an invisible someone using his foot ordered me to get up as I was hindering disembarkation.

Boulogne Rest Camp

On the 9th July 1915 at 2am, we docked. It was a slow process getting our feet on *terra firma* and as we were not the only unit on board, there was an inevitable delay before the whole battalion was eventually lined up on the quay. Just as it was turning daylight, we marched off full of enthusiasm and when we got out of the harbour we let everyone know we had arrived by opening up with "Camerons Egorrah" (have I spelt it right?). This may or may not be our war cry but it went something like this:

> *A la saVa .... A la saVa*
> *The CO rah bel ....The CO rah bel*
> *Ching..... ching..... Chingoooooooo*
> *Camerons e Go rah Camerons e Go rah*
> *e Go rah.. e Go rah ....GOOOOOO rah*

It could not have been sung other than with gusto and that was sufficient to arouse those within hearing distance.

Who should refrain from wanting to join in if only they knew the words?

With our immaculately attired pipers and drummers leading, up the hill we went, surveyed, mostly, by women and children at their open-outward windows. They gave us a rapturous welcome, despite their having been awakened by our enthusiastic pipe band. One or two white-aproned café owners and waiters standing at doorways, animated the scene by waving serviettes. Very rarely did we see other than elderly men.

In addition to the rough and sleepless night on the channel crossing, climbing up that hilly street was quite an ordeal and some of us were no doubt sorry that we had crammed little extras into our packs and haversacks, thereby adding to the already heavy weight of our equipment.

Slightly fatigued, we completed our climb to be confronted with an array of bell-tents. This was the Rest Camp through which the infantry passed. There was an almost inconspicuous entrance to it, and practically nothing to prevent sightseers from encroaching on this camp, particularly at the rear. Most of those who did so were teenagers and children hunting for souvenirs. Bully beef was in great demand and had apparently been freely distributed by our predecessors.

Straying a little, I had the opportunity of airing my schoolboy French – much to the amusement of the youngsters who were trying me out. It was quite a pleasant change to fraternise with such a mixed and inquisitive audience but as the numbers increased, I and the others were ordered back to camp.

The town centre was placed 'out of bounds' and that disappointed those hopefuls who wanted to see the sights and visit the cafes to get a taste of the French life.

CHAPTER 8 – [1915]

To the Western Front

We were in the Rest Camp for one night only. On the 10th July 1915 we went by train to Watten Eperleque – a mere 'halt' in open country. It was more like a 'fun ride' – for behind the engine, which was frequently blotted out by either steam or smoke, was a train of squeaky wagons, on each of which was clearly painted "10 CHEVAUX (or was it 8?) OU 40 HOMMES" – in other words 'ten horses or forty men'. Standing or squatting on a partially open 'goods' train, added to the novelty of our first railway experience in France as soldiers.

The speed, at times, was laughable. For instance, if you were in the last wagon, you could get off, run along the track until you reached the engine, mount without protest from the driver, and get your 'dixie' filled with hot water. Then it was simply a case of dismounting and waiting for your wagon to arrive, then scrambling onto it to enjoy your brew!

After a brief halt at Watten Eperleque, we started out on 'Shanks's pony' through the Pas De Calais. The *Routes*

Nationales, generally lined on both sides by exceptionally tall plane trees, were indisputably ideal highways for mechanised transport. For soldiers on foot, however, it was an entirely different matter. Although the foliage afforded welcome shade from the hot sun, the road surface was the worst one imaginable for marching on with a heavy pack, as the square, slightly convex cobblestones offered grip before the feet – in fact, the opposite. (This type of road came into being in the days before the motor car, and was designed so that the caulks on horseshoes would minimise the risk of the animals slipping). From the soldiers' point of view, any other road surface would have been preferable. There were no pavements, but plenty verdure if one wanted to rest for a while in comfort without being inconvenienced.

I was practically the last man in the battalion, and was thoroughly enjoying a long overdue "Halt, Fall out..." for a rest and a Woodbine or Richmond Gem, when I was more than surprised to hear the following:

"Private Burns of 'D' Company to report to the Colonel at the Double!"

When I arrived at the head of the column, I was told that as I had been seen having a conversation with civilians at Boulogne Rest Camp. No doubt, I could speak French. Agreeing to this assertion, I was thereupon instructed to accompany a Captain Davy (GAC) and assist him in finding billets when we reached Houlle.

For me, this unexpected assignment not only put a feather in my cap, but I was sure it would be an interesting experience. It certainly was. Unfortunately, my services as an interpreter did not last long as a Liaison Officer in French uniform came and took over.

One of our billets was a farm and like most farms it had out-houses on three sides: byres, stables, barns etc, with private quarters overlooking the courtyard in the centre.

This centre of the courtyard was the depository – a favourite resort for the chickens and ducks and small four-legged nocturnal prowlers along with swarms of buzzing pests – all thoroughly enjoying themselves in and around the smell sludge (phew!).

It was just getting dark and we were given freedom in picking a place to sleep. The over-eager, hoping to get the best niches, took a short-cut and unwittingly found themselves "up to their knees in it". Afterwards, they came squelching and complaining and permeating our barn with obnoxious odours.

In the corner of the barn I earmarked a reasonably clean and spacious spot for myself, and, taking fresh hay from a manger, made myself a comfortable stretch-out. Remembering how I had lost my bed in Inverness, I stayed put until it appeared that all the others in that barn were settled in.

Unfortunately, I didn't realise that up in the rafters, the barn had a number of other inhabitants. They cackled, cooed, cheeped and cock-a-doodle-dooed throughout the night and early morning. No proper eggs were forthcoming, but there were lots of others – without shells. I was lucky that there were no 'feathered friends' directly above my bivouac. In the morning, several of the other lads had considerable difficulty restoring themselves to the condition expected of a member of the Shiny Seventh!

At another small farm which we commandeered, there were no menfolk – just a woman who was striving to increase her stock. Unfortunately her stock bull did not appear to be up to the job, either in size or experience. Our soldiers-cum-stud-hands needed no encouragement when invited to help solve the difficulties. Scouting around, they found a spare door and improvised an upward slope behind 'Clarabelle'. It was then possible for John Bull (or perhaps that should be Jean Bull) to complete his mission. *Merci beaucoup!*

On the 12th July 1915 (only three days after our arrival in France) whilst still at Houlle, we had another inspection – this time by Field Marshal Sir John French.

On the 15th July 1915 we marched to Hazebrouk – about 20 miles – where we spent the night. The following day it was on to Gonnehem then Houchin (17th) through to Mazingarbe to Les Brebis (18th) where we remained a few days before returning to Houchin.

Most of these movements, necessitating long marches, took place in darkness to avoid being spotted by the enemy. It being summertime, this meant marching between midnight and daybreak. Our arrival at our new destination was followed by the inevitable scramble for a place to stretch out.

The further we marched, the more intense became the rumble of shellfire and the 'crunches' of the high explosive shells. What looked like shooting stars in the distance, were actually the Verey Lights put up by both sides – usually a sign of nervousness – which indicated we were now not far from the 'front line'.

CHAPTER 9 – [1915]

The Firing Line

It's now the 28th July and gradually 'broken in'. As we thread our way through the debris of an abandoned village and the courtyard of what was once a farm it's 'heads down' all the time as there is so much stuff flying around.

One by one we scramble into a 'communication trench' that has been severely damaged. Instead of the seven feet deep it should have been it is only two or three feet in places – totally insufficient to afford us any protection.

It was sheer madness on the part of the inquisitive to stick their heads over the parapet to try and see 'where they were'. As it turned out, this forward movement was just to give us an idea what we would be facing in the very near future. After two days at the front line we would return to Houchin.

However, in our innocence we found these two days really exciting, as soon as we realised where we were. Everyone was soon asking: "Where are the Germans?"

The question was quickly answered when up went a string of Verey Lights which lit up 'No Man's Land'.

Soon it was a case of 'off we go again'. It was 2ⁿᵈ August, almost a year since the declaration of war. I remembered the often repeated headlines in the national press that stated: 'ALL QUIET ON THE WESTERN FRONT'. I was now in a position to see and hear for myself if such reports were merely bluff…

It was daylight when we started to go up to the front, but after having to zig-zag our way around or over so many obstacles in the much-battered communication trenches, in addition to taking cover from time to time because of the intermittent shell bursts, it was dark before we got into the front line at Maroc.

No playing at soldiers now – we had actually taken over a section of the 'firing line' where we must be continually on the *qui vive* (who goes there?).

At intervals along the trench, a man was given a post on the 'fire step' for lookout purposes. Imagine his surprise at seeing, a hundred yards or so in front of us, makeshift notices which read: "Why shoot? We are Saxons and you are Anglo-Saxons." Unbelievable! Had the Germans got the wind up? Perhaps it was because they knew that they were now confronted by the 'Ladies from Hell'.

Here in the Maroc section of the line, I found that I was in rather a unique position. I was the 'right hand man' – that is to say, the man to the extreme right of our company's position. As I was in 'D' Company in 16 platoon – the rearmost platoon in an infantry regiment – I was possibly the man on the extreme right of the entire British Expeditionary Force in France!

This would appear to be indisputable as I found myself fraternising with French soldiers who assured me that they were on the extreme left of their army's position.

Soon we began swapping souvenirs. Cigarettes (Woodbine, Hill's Campaigner, Richmond Gem) were freely given and exchanged for Gauloises, whilst bully beef and MacConnochie rations seemed a fair swap for French red wine and cheese. We were curious to observe that many Froggies had a lighter made out of a spent cartridge, complete with a foot-long wick.

The French soldiers carried identity papers in their wallets and took a delight in showing us photographs of their families. (Having been in the French version of what we would call the Territorial Army, they were not young and many of them had families.)

A feature that was noticeable about their heavy uniform was that the bottom part of the front of their greatcoats could be fastened up in order to permit greater freedom of leg movement – which would be very useful when on the march. (Luckily for them, they did not have bare knees as we Scots did).

This mutually happy surprise get-together was unfortunately to be short-lived as we were soon relieved by the Seaforths. They, like ourselves, were alternating between the firing line and the support trenches as were the other battalions in our brigade. This was always preferable to being too long in one place.

It had been rather quiet and it was a relief to see planes hovering around. If they were German, we had every opportunity to show our skill as marksmen, for the pilot or gunner could be plainly seen. We were always ready to have a go at them with either a rifle or a revolver when their open-cockpit planes were seen approaching us. Frequently there would be an exceptionally low-flying plane with a cameraman who would no doubt be endeavouring to photograph details of our observation posts etc. They did not all get back. Several of them went crashing behind our lines before finishing in a cloud of smoke.

One curious point was that on night patrols or sorties, men were prohibited from wearing watches with luminous dials. It was, therefore, not uncommon to see someone with his wristwatch enclosed in a khaki-coloured hinged metal case. Perhaps these had been specially made for night-patrol purposes, but as time went on they became quite common.

On one of our early visits to the Front Line we were very close to the enemy trenches. There was sometimes an amusing interlude when up would go a few German bayonets each with a helmet swinging on top, presumably to entice our snipers to indulge in a bit of rifle practice? In friendly appreciation of their prank, up would go a Cameron bayonet with an empty Woodbine tin as a target.

It was surprisingly peaceful. No indiscriminate rifle fire or trench mortars to disturb those who were trying to get a nap after spending hours during the night on 'look-out' duty. Now and again the Germans exhibit their notices about our Anglo-Saxon relationship.

On a summer's day what could be more comforting and reassuring than to watch the skylarks and other birds as they flutter between the trenches – where no man dares to tread?

The trenches we are in are much wider than those we occupied in Reserve, and thanks to the dry weather lately we can move around without difficulty. During the rainy season it was a case of having to struggle just to get one's feet out of the mud.

In some trenches, particularly communications trenches, duckboards were introduced. They were supposed to prevent us from sinking into the mud, but unfortunately, in wet weather they became very slippery, and as the rain and mud accumulated on them the more hazardous they became, as they were not fixed and were easily displaced. Therefore they were something of a failure, because in the dry weather they were superfluous whereas in bad weather their usefulness was questionable.

Whilst negotiating the various trenches, one would frequently hear a cry of "Heads down – aerial cable!" This meant that we had to keep our rifles or whatever we were carrying down in order to avoid interfering with the telephone wires laid by the Signallers. Every forward move necessitated additional lines – new ones – as the exigencies of the service did not warrant collecting, adapting or repairing those in any way defective. It was absolutely imperative that there be uninterrupted communication between the front line and the rear. In addition, the artillery observation posts up front had their own separate lines. It will be appreciated therefore that with so many cables of various colours, every care had to be taken not to jeopardise their serviceability.

After only a few days in the firing line, we went back to Maroc and on to Mazingarbe and into billets – to rest, presumably.

There was invariably some work to be done, such as tidying up the streets or filling in shell-holes and re-making battered reserve and communication trenches – anything to keep up our morale, even at the expense of sapping our energy.

When we came back to a village to rest it was customary to post a sentry on guard outside the Company or Battalion Headquarters – whether a chateau, a school or farmhouse. Of course, a kilted sentry, whether standing at "attention" or "at ease", was always the centre of attention – more so in a village not previously occupied by the "Jocks".

Just picture, if you will, a six-foot-tall Highlander, standing at the entrance to Headquarters, bayonet gleaming, forbidden to enter into conversation with the friendly but curious local people, surrounded by a crowd of small children peering at his bare knees and short 'skirt'!

On one occasion, one of our stalwarts turned up after sentry duty with a bleeding chin, and we were curious to learn how this injury came about. We had just been relieved in the trenches and had come back for a much-needed rest. Unfortunately for him, although completely worn out, he was picked for sentry duty.

Knowing that for a sentry to fall asleep on duty – especially on active service – was regarded as one of the most serious of crimes, he decided to take no risk. When it was dark he stood with the point of his bayonet under his chin, just in case he started to nod off – which of course he did – with painful consequences!

I discovered that volunteers were being sought to undergo a course in signalling, and didn't hesitate in putting my name down. After being interviewed, I was fortunate enough to be considered suitable. Consequently, whilst the rank and file were slogging away at fatigues or doing exercises, I was having a cushy time of it indoors learning how to send messages using Morse code, or by flag-wagging to other signallers stationed a long way off.

Semaphore was certainly preferable as a means of communication, as it entailed carrying only two flags, whereas signalling with Morse meant we had to lug around a small contraption like a car battery – and it certainly wasn't lightweight! I became proficient in both categories and was duly earmarked to be appointed as a Company Signaller when we returned to the front line.

There was one fellow who intrigued us in many ways and his imperturbable demeanour left us guessing as to what he might have done in Civvy Street. One of the most curious aspects of his behaviour was the way in which he shaved himself in the morning. With a 5 x 4 inch steel mirror tied to the adjustable bracket on the skylight window in the loft of a farm where we were resting, we watched him one morning as he proceeded with his bizarre shaving ritual. We made no comment, as with each sweep of his chin or cheek, he would wipe the soap off the open razor on to his hairy head. One of our more la-de-da stockbroker types looked on in amazement and gave the impression that he was shocked at seeing a man wiping a dirty razor on his head and did not hesitate to say so. However, the la-de-da quickly withdrew into his scabbard when the other chap retorted:

"Look here you. I have just done five years in the clink and if you would like to know, that's where I learnt this trick. Don't forget, every time I shave like this I am bound to wash my head immediately afterwards. If you did the same you would not be so lousy... Just try it!"

❖ ❖ ❖

When in Mazingarbe a few of us always made a bee-line to a comfortable little establishment at the corner of one of the streets. (Surprisingly, despite their proximity to the front line, this and other shops were still bravely trying to carry on.)

In this particular café there were never more than a dozen people – all old folk – and three or four attentive females behind the bar or in the kitchen. We indulged in our favourite drink – Grenadine – which was not expensive for those who we hoped would invite us to 'have a drink with them'.

When it was time to go, we said "olive oil" (*au revoir*) and indulged in friendly embraces, with a promise that we would be back one day. Not wishing to 'put the wind up them' we nevertheless advised all in the establishment that it would be wise to get out of the village in the interests of their own safety. However, they seemed determined to remain, in the hope of hanging on to their possessions. They assured us that, if necessary, they would take shelter in the wine cellars!

❖ ❖ ❖

We left Mazingarbe on the 10th August and for the next few weeks made short visits to the front line. On the 12th September we went into billets at Verquin. Mine was the lowest grade possible; I had to sleep on a stone floor. Because we had to be continually on the alert, I was fully clad overnight except for my boots. These I placed toe-to-toe, so as to provide a cradle-like pillow for my head.

On the 21st September, our gunners seemed to have gone berserk, for it was pandemonium all day long. Darkness was falling when we got into trenches at Verquin and we laboriously threaded our way up to Vermelles.

Our accumulating mail had at last been brought to us, but scarcely had distribution been completed when the bugle call for "Fall In" came, leaving those who were last to receive their mail, little time to open their long overdue parcels or read the news from home. Carrying a heavy pack was bad enough, but with the addition of food parcels, it was not easy negotiating so many obstacles in narrow and damaged communication trenches, all the time having to take evasive action from the many shell-bursts.

The further up we went the heavier the barrage became – just as if it was a preconceived plan by the Germans to let us come right up and then "let us have it".

However, our Artillery was doing a smashing job also. Passing a camouflaged gun-pit, I stopped momentarily to watch the non-stop loading and firing of the big shells. Sleeves rolled up and perspiring, the gunners' movements were almost mechanical. It was evident that I was interested, but I got a surprise when one of the gunners said to me, his eyes on my parcels, "You'll not need those where you are going".

As I was already exhausted, I opened one of my parcels and handed over some small tins of foodstuffs, so as to lighten the load. However, I kept several hundred cigarettes that had been sent all the way from Canada with a note from my uncle inviting me out for a holiday when the war was over! We moved on to 'Quality Street' and waited there until it was time to slide into the trenches.

The Battle of Loos

Whiz-bang! Whiz-bang! And so it went on, on this early morning of the 25th September 1915. In a rising mist, the Battle of Loos had been launched. Our front line trench, from the protective point of view, was absolutely useless on account of the retaliatory action by the Germans to our 'softening-up' artillery barrage prior to the pending attack.

Having squeezed our way out of the damaged dug-out we waited for that fateful word: "Advance".

When this order was finally given at 6am, I experienced no difficulty in getting up and over the parapet. Small ladders had been provided to facilitate our getting out of our front line trench, although, owing to its battered condition and they were not really necessary as it was quite an easy matter to climb up unaided.

So for the first time, the 7th Camerons with fixed bayonets went 'over the top' – but to what?

Wherever he was, I could not see him, but a Piper, in accordance with tradition was there to inspire us; he may even have belonged to the Black Watch. Because of the awful gunfire noises it was only occasionally we could hear the mournful drone of the pipes.

We noticed a really horrible sickly smell. It would go away and then come back again in invisible waves – it was gas!

Those who did not put on their masks, unfortunately eventually fell victims to its effects. I shouted to one fellow who was in difficulties, "Put on your mask!", but he said that when it was on he could not breathe – which meant that his mask must be defective – and he continued coughing.

At first we thought the gas was released by the enemy, but we later learned that our own side was responsible for its use. It was no doubt anticipated that the direction of the wind (although there was none, as far as I can recall) would carry it over to the German lines. (What was it my namesake said about "The best laid schemes of mice and men"?)

In addition to the firing and the flashes from the French 75s (captured by the Germans early in the war) there was the incessant spluttering and cracking of machine gun fire coming from different directions, accompanied by showers of earth and other miscellany thrown up by the frequent HE explosions.

Having wriggled through, over or under masses of barbed wire – which was responsible for many casualties – we threaded our way out of the much damaged village of Loos.

It was here that I experienced the first real horror of war. I was running like mad over No Man's Land with another fellow (whether he was Black Watch or Cameron I could not say) practically rubbing shoulders with me. There was a flash and a bang and I threw myself to the ground. When I got up and looked around I found myself alone. It seemed impossible, but my companion had simply vanished. I was shocked, but nevertheless I did not broadcast what I had experienced.

Making our way forward, slowly now, over the churned-up ground and skirting the water-filled shell-holes, I and my little bunch of stalwarts were astonished to see a group of Germans coming out of a knock-about haystack – all with their hands up. Having been cut off by our incessant shelling, they appeared very pleased to be taken prisoner. It was obvious that the haystack had been used as an observation post. Behind it there was a most commodious dugout complete with telephones. Its existence explained how the Germans had been aware of our preparations for the attack.

With Loos now behind us, we pushed forward up and up to the top of Hill 70. With the mist completely gone, from where we were we had a clear view of the war-torn panorama with pit-heads in the distance.

On each side of us, though some way off, we could distinguish 'Jocks' on the move. It seemed that the whole Highland Brigade was engaged in this action.

Our objective – I was to learn much later – was to press on through Cité St Auguste, which was not far off, without stopping 'until we get there'. Unfortunately it appeared that, wherever 'there' was, no-one seemed to know.

How on earth was it going to be possible to break through that stretch of barbed wire immediately in front of us? All anticipated obstacles were supposed to have been demolished by our Artillery which had been very active during the past few days and nights. However, there we lay on top of Hill 70, facing the enemy, whose guns, on either side of the wire defences, were 'whiz-banging' non-stop, supplemented by more heavy artillery from further back. What was going to happen now that we were stuck?

I was lying beside Captain Cameron, our Company Commander – a small but much respected officer. There was no NCO near and he said to me:

"We've got to do something. I want you to go back to Battalion Headquarters in Loos village."

He wrote a message and gave it to me with orders to locate Colonel Sandilands. In case something happened to me, I tucked the message between my wrist and my watch and cautiously made my way back up the hill, fully aware of the fact that the higher I went the easier it would be for me to be spotted by the Germans, especially as I was on the move. Through sheer fatigue (or was it due to fright?) I lay down on my stomach frequently for a few minutes, fully aware that if I stood up I would be liable to 'stop one'.

I decided that the time was not opportune to make a dash for it, and was therefore greatly relieved when at last I succeeded in getting over the brow of the hill and out of sight of the enemy, who had been putting down a hail of shells which menaced all those on and near the hill as well as those in proximity to the village. Now, I thought, it would not be too difficult to fulfil my mission.

In front of the village – which was now badly battered – I came across a cluster of 'brass hats' – their epaulettes adorned with stars, crowns and cross-swords. They were standing in a slit trench about twenty feet long, facing the front line and scanning various maps which were laid out on the waist-high ground before them.

Out of breath and saluting them, I informed them that I had just come from the firing line with a very important message for Colonel Sandilands of the 7th Cameron

Highlanders. All I got by way of an answer was – "He's not here... try the village somewhere".

I thought that, in view of their high rank, they might have taken the appropriate action right away, in ordering our artillery to destroy the wire defences which were impeding our progress and at the same time knock out the small guns which we could clearly see from the top of the Hill. If they had done so, perhaps we could have continued with our forward thrust.

Where could I find my CO? I scouted round but no help was forthcoming from the many stragglers in the village as to the location of our battalion headquarters. My anxiety was growing with every passing minute. Because of the frequent bursts of shrapnel in the village the 'lost' men were chiefly intent on taking cover – all except the brave stretcher bearers who were conscientiously attending to the many causalities.

It was gruesome to see dead horses and even worse listening to the neighing of the wounded ones still in harness. There was only one humane thing to do with the latter and I was pleased to see them put out of their misery by sympathetic soldiers in the absence of members of the RVC.

It was very disturbing not to be able to hand over my message, as all the time I had it with me, I was thinking of my pals up there on the hill in full view of the enemy. Coming across an opening in a heap of ruins, I looked in and saw some steps leading down into darkness. It would have been an ideal place for headquarters… but no.

Going down the steps very cautiously I heard human voices and was flabbergasted to faintly see German soldiers. They stood with 'hands up' at a table upon which was one solitary candle. Whatever they said I could not understand. They probably thought there were others behind me and seemed resigned to the fact that they were now prisoners – no doubt they considered themselves lucky to be in a safe place. Somehow, I managed to keep my *sang froid* and with no knowledge whatsoever of German except "gooden dag" or something like that, I retraced by steps.

Relieved to get away from those Germans, I came across a handful of men quite near and excitedly shouted to them that there were some Huns with 'hands up' awaiting collection! Thrilled to bits, and with bayonets fixed, down they went and very soon afterwards, up came the frightened prisoners. What happened to them I do not know, nor was I interested at the time, for I was still anxious to find our own Headquarters, which I was assured were somewhere in Loos village.

Spotting a horse sniffing around and no one near it, I went over and commandeered it. It had a bridle with a rope for reins, but no saddle. What a spectacle! A kilty riding a bareback horse! Nevertheless, this enabled me to move about quicker and I eventually met up with a Scottish Officer to whom I handed over Captain Cameron's message, emphasising the difficulties I had encountered, including my brush-off by the 'brass hats'.

Now rid of my responsibility and feeling rather sore and glad to get off that flea-infested bunch of bones, I made my way, unhurriedly I admit, back to report to my Captain.

"The higher up, the better the scenery" they say, and as I looked to the rear I could see, not far away, the cavalry drawn up in such a manner as to suggest that the squadron was about to move up. In fact, when we had broken through the German lines it was intended, I believe, that the cavalry would continue the rout, supported by the mass of infantry stationed in the background.

When I regained the top of Hill 70 I was surprised to see some of our men still there. During my unexpected experience as a messenger it was evident that our lads had been digging in for all they were worth in order to hold on to what they had won. There was no sign of Captain Cameron. What happened to him during the time we were held up in front of the unbroken barbed wire?

From the elevated position I had a clear view of the enemy's defences immediately in front of us and of Germans exposing themselves when moving around the gun-pits. The 75s and the Heavies were very active, their flashes revealing just how many there were.

George was lying on his stomach, his two feet alternating in upward and downward movements. I asked him what was the big idea and he coolly replied that he "wanted one in the leg" so as to get back to Blighty before he got completely bumped off like some of the others! We all agreed when discussing casualties that it was much better to get 'one in the leg' than risk getting it elsewhere.

Exhausted by digging in to provide maximum protection in case of a counter-attack, it was no picnic up there as we were being subjected to outbursts of shrapnel coming from more than one direction.

It had been a long day in that red-hot area and when darkness came we managed, with difficulty, to get back to a relatively safe spot at Philosophe early in the morning. We jumped for joy at finding our Field Kitchens where we were given hot tea and a very big helping of rum before attacking the grub.

An initial roll-call was made, but, alas, there were only about 75 out of the whole battalion who had found their way back to where we now were. As the hours passed quite a few more turned up, but it was pitiful to see the condition in which they were 'staggering home'.

Then the innumerable questions, such as "When or where did you see so-and-so last?" or "did you actually leave anyone killed or wounded?" I was too overcome to give details of what I had seen and limited my contribution on this inquest by relating how I found "G.B." I gave him a drink and left my bottle beside him hoping that someone else would be able to help, if he was found in time.

I did no forget that we had strict instructions never to stop and tend the wounded as it was the duty of the stretcher bearers to follow up and do whatever was necessary. It was clearly emphasised that our job was to keep going until we reached our objective.

Our stop in Philosophe was welcome, but short, for within a few hours we were humping it back to Quality Street and into a Support Line. What had been well maintained trenches before the battle was now a quagmire. Thankfully, we were quickly relieved and once again made our way to Mazingarbe where we remained for a couple of days.

That was the Battle of Loos – a short but disastrous action. It was our first real experience of 'kill or be killed' and it was revealed later that our losses of killed or missing were between five and six hundred – a day of merciless slaughter of man and beast.

When 'nice n' comfy' in Mazingarbe again we made a point of looking for the café where we had supped our Grenadine and said "au revoir" to the brave villagers and the three women who served us and gave us such a friendly welcome despite the hazardous conditions under which they were striving to keep going. But the village must have had a right good strafing during our absence, for the buildings were almost completely razed. We eventually found what was left of the café, but it had every appearance of having received a direct hit. None of us had the pluck to examine the cellar and in any case, it would have required a Herculean effort to remove the debris over the entrance to it. Were the barmaids trapped down below?

Shells were still falling haphazardly and we were constantly on the alert. Two came in quick succession, not nose-cap first as was generally the case, but landed on their sides, most fortunately for us, and scudded along the main 'street' at umpteen miles an hour, giving us time to take cover before they came into contact with something, when it was 'bang, bang and upsadaisy' followed by our relieved comments along the lines of "at least my name's not on that one!"

Until I mounted that filthy old horse in Loos, I had never been bothered by fleas or lice. However, in Mazingarbe I was forced to attend to my 'wardrobe' and was able to benefit from a piece of advice that I had been given. I dug a hole in the ground two inches deep and about one yard square. I took off my kilt by removing the one and only safety pin and spread it out in the hole, covering it over with top soil and leaving it there for over an hour. (Fortunately, it was not cold on this late September day). The trick had worked, for on minute examination not a living flea or louse could be seen.

After a comparatively easy time we marched to Lillers – a tidy town with an imposing Mairie and an extensive place which accommodated the weekly markets and the fetes for the local area. We had a terrific welcome and in view of what we had been through recently, seeing so many civilians – of both sexes – lifted our morale considerably.

I was billeted in a private house in the town centre – Rue de Sebastopol – where I enjoyed the undreamed of luxury of a hot bath to soak the dry mud off my hairy legs, and hot food served at a table instead of dry biscuits and rainwater eaten in an open trench. I was pleased that I had got rid of the fleas before coming here! I was the only soldier in the house of Madame Dupont and her two tiny children whose father was "somewhere at the front". No matter where we went – even in a half-demolished village – the people were exceptionally attentive to us and seemed to derive much pleasure in making us 'dooz oof et pang' – otherwise known as two eggs with several inches of baguette.

During my rest periods, my chief pleasure was writing home, giving vivid details of my exploits, without divulging anything that could have been useful to the enemy.

In addition, I took the opportunity of dropping a line or a postcard to a few of the civilians who had been kind to me, but on only two occasions did I give an address, which was 7th Cameron Highlanders, 15th Scottish Division, B.E.F. whereupon replies reached me without signs of having been opened.

Sometimes when writing home, if there was a Bureau de Poste in the village or town, I would not hesitate in buying stamps and posting my letters in the ordinary way – just as a civilian would do. I made enquiries and found that each letter got to its destination without any sign of interference by the authorities. When I look back on these instances, I find it absolutely astonishing that censorship regulations permitted such loopholes to exist.

For ordinary correspondence our letters were put in addressed unsealed envelopes – supposedly to be censored by one of the company officers. From what I gathered, having satisfied himself that the writer hadn't given away any secrets, the officer would seal the envelope, add his initials, then have them passed on to the Field Post Office.

Periodically, about once a month, we were given a Green Envelope. The contents of these were not to refer to anything other than matters of a strictly private nature. The envelopes, sealed by the writer, did not have to be examined by a company officer. So far as I was concerned none of my letters had been subjected to censorship before reaching their destinations. These Green Envelopes were in great demand (more particularly by married men) and were willingly exchanged for fags.

Now the 12th October 1915 the luxury of a rest period had come to an end. We got a train to Noeux Les Mines where we stayed before going into the trenches a fortnight later. There we took over the captured Germans trenches before going into Reserve, then up again to the Front, switching all the time until handing over prior to our returning to billets at Philosophe.

Not for long, however, and on the 16th November it was 'up' once more to go to the Front Line.

As soon as we got into the communication trenches a bombardment opened up and continued even when we had taken over – seemingly as if the enemy's intelligence was aware of what was happening.

Everyone who had survived and had 'done' this part of the Line will remember the coal mine with the two-wheel shaft-head overlooking the body-strewn battlefield. Here we were once again under its shadow, surprised to find that this landmark had withstood so many incessant bombardments. Undoubtedly it was an important Observation Post – responsible for our heavy casualties two months ago.

At this time of year the days were getting shorter and the weather was adding to our discomfort and difficulties. The rain had necessitated the shoring up of the sides of the trenches and making new fire-steps – not easy when one is handicapped by gluey mud.

Whenever an HE shell exploded near us, the roof of our dugout or lean-to would collapse depriving us of any protection from the elements or from that which went up and had to come down.

On account of being so far forward and in newly conquered trenches there were no duck-boards and with the rain responsible for the ankle-deep quagmire, plus overnight frost, no wonder so many men had to be taken to hospital suffering from 'trench foot'.

Irrespective of weather conditions there was always something happening – day and night – but daytime antics of a few Taubes afforded us a welcome diversion if they came near enough to warrant rapid fire from our rifles or Lewis guns.

Frequently there would be a dull sort of 'plump' coming from enemy lines. Looking skyward and if not too far away one could see a "Minnenwerfer" soaring several hundred feet. Shaped like a football with an eighteen inch (approximately) shaft on it, the contrivance would gradually lose momentum, twirl round and round with the ball part now coming down first hitting a blind target with one mighty crunch. Then up would go whatever it struck – provided it was not a dud. If it landed on something solid the explosion would be deafening, but if in a nearby water filled shell-hole not so pronounced, when perhaps we would escape with just a shower of mud and water. We always prayed it would not find a latrine or our improvised kitchen.

One consolation in daytime was that as it could be spotted on its way up and down, it was sometimes possible to vamoose either to the right or to the left to get away from the likely landing spot.

Four weeks after vacating Philosophe we were alternating between the Firing Line and Reserve with very brief period in billets either at Noeux Les Mines, Sailly la Bourse, Noyelles, not overlooking another tour at Philosphe.

Most of these recent moves entailed long marches – very exhausting over shell-torn roads – and full equipment to add to our troubles.

In and out of German trenches at various part of the Front, I picked up many little pests and I was always delighted when it was made known that a bathing parade was being arranged.

In some situations there were several pit-heads around so there were no difficulties in being provided with a first-class service as the miners had all the facilities available to them after completing their shift.

Whilst on the subject of 'bathing' I recall one occasion when we were escorted to a garage-like building where, placed a few feet apart, were quite a hundred ordinary shallow washtubs with steaming water into which the RMAC Orderlies were sprinkling disinfectant. With what I found in the German trenches, combined with memories of that flea-infested horse at Loos, I reckoned I needed an extra dose of whatever was being poured into my tub and I had no hesitation in scrounging a wee drop more. With a queer look, accompanied by subdued giggle, the orderly willingly obliged. I regretted my greed and indiscretion and soon found myself performing "The Dance of the Nudes" round my bath tub, yelling my head off – much to the amusement of others! My discomfort was not temporary for I suffered a burning sensation for many hours afterwards.

On the 14th December we left Philosophe and hiked it to Noeux Les Mines where we were glad to get on to a train which took us to Lillers from where we walked on to Allouagne.

I was very fortunate in being billeted c/o Madame Poness, Rue Du Pont.

We had quite a lengthy stay in this, almost undisturbed little town. Being Christmas time we joined the locals in the celebrations. On Christmas Day a boxing match took place in the open air. It was just the thing for 'he men' – a Cameron trying to knock out a Seaforth – but it was not to be. As for New Year's Eve and New Year's Day, the celebrations were very much in accordance with Scottish tradition.

From Allouague we set out on long marches, taking in many tiny villages including Auchy, Rely, Coyecque, Billery, Hurionville and Burdure returning to Allouague on 7th January (now 1916).

Thus we had four weeks miles away from the activities and hardships of the Front Line.

Alas, on the 14th January we returned to Loos and Hill 70 where we had suffered such heavy losses only about four months previously.

What a surprise! Who were these men coming into our trenches? None other that the 6th Royal Irish. They were certainly 'green' for they had joined us to be 'broken in'

It was a welcome break to have a bit of Blarney and it gave us the opportunity to 'show off', although they did not relish some of the tales we related about what had happened to us four months previously, almost at the same spot.

As "Paddy" had not hitherto been up to the Front, he could not understand why we didn't get on with the job instead of hanging around waiting for something to happen.

We had our anxious moments preventing some of these dare-devils from exposing themselves to the enemy in order to see what was over there on the other side of the barbed wire aligning the parapets. At daybreak along came the Rum Ration – eagerly awaited by most. Supervised by a Lieutenant, the platoon sergeant had the job of pouring a little into the lid of a dixie – shakily extended by a frozen hand. I told the Officer I did not drink but the sergeant tersely informed me "orders is orders – drink it". I waited a few minutes until he was out of sight so that I could pass it on to someone.

"Paddy" had evidently overheard the conversation with the officer as he wasted no time 'at all at all' in volunteering to drink my ration "as it was the next best thing to whisky". Willingly I acceded to his pleading and he wasted no time in gulping it down.

He asked, once again, how long we had been wasting our time standing around here doing nothing. Then immediately, pushing us aside, he became excited and adopting an obstreperous attitude shouted "I'll show you how to kill these ******* Germans!" He grabbed his rifle, jumped up on the fire-step and looked over the parapet. Sadly, before we managed to pull him down there came a burst of machine gun fire and he fell back into the trench.

With regard to the rum, the jars were kept in a dugout near which I was squatted ready for my buzzer to go. The platoon sergeant asked me to keep my eye on these for a minute. I kept them under rigid surveillance until who should come along but a sergeant-major. "Where is the rum?" he asked and all I could reply was that I was instructed by my sergeant not to let anyone have it. The sergeant-major authoritatively left me in no doubt as to who gave the so-and-so orders in this battalion. I could do no more than watch while he took several swigs of it and after a "that's that" along the trench he went. I never saw him again. Was he reduced to the ranks? I never knew.

The wintry conditions were really horrible and in addition to being drenched due to the lack of dug-outs, the front line trenches were like a quagmire – 'up to the knees' in mud. Having bare knees it was advisable to wipe off the mud before it hardened.

For several days, a white mist enshrouded our sector, visibility being down to a few yards. On one such day we seized the opportunity of going up over the parapets to stretch our legs

Out of sight of the enemy we scouted round in the hope of discovering something unusual, but what did we see? Corpses, some with and others without kilts, shreds of various tartans hanging limply from the barbed wire. There were more in the murky water of the shell-holes – it was a gruesome sight. We searched for identity discs or documents in the saturated uniforms but could find no clues for us to hand over.

Scattered about were machine guns, rifles, gas masks and equipment. Rusty and muddy; it did not seem worthwhile salvaging anything.

It would have been imprudent to take too many liberties and an occasional bullet whizzing past in the rising mist was sufficient to warrant our beating a hasty retreat to our squelching trench.

What I had seen was very disheartening and in addition to being cold I was starving. Fortunately, Fate was good to me. My pal Jimmy, who was a scout attached to battalion headquarters, frequently came up to the firing line with messages for various officers, and on these occasions he invariably brought me a flask of hot tea and bits of things to eat, taking the thermos flask back with him for use on subsequent errands.

Whilst on the subject of food, I recall how we managed in the firing line. Some of us had our own "field kitchen" – a little niche, eye level, about a foot square, burrowed into the side of the trench. In this we had our heating apparatus – a small wax night-light or bits of candles, over which we held or propped up our dixies. It was a very slow method, but with patience we managed to get the water sufficiently hot to melt an Oxo cube or to make tea (sugarless). What could have been more palatable than either of these with the addition of Cleeve's condensed milk!

Where did the water come from? Simple, when it rained we made a 'reservoir' by opening our ground sheet (rubber one side with eyelets all round) and arranging it in such a manner so as to catch sufficient for our immediate requirements.

Alas! There were catastrophes, for there were occasions when over would come an HE or other projectile which would explode in the vicinity causing a minor 'earthquake' nullifying all our efforts and dashing our hopes. When there was no hostile interference, however, these alfresco interludes bridged over many a craving and provided a worthwhile diversion.

How does one manage to pass the time when there is a lull? Sometimes it is inexplicably boring but if there is a pack of cards it is great fun trying to make a few francs at 'banker' etc.

Killing rats was more exciting. On throwing some of our 'iron' biscuits on the ground there would be an immediate and adventurous sortie of huge and small rats squealing and fighting amongst themselves for possession, seemingly oblivious to our presence, until – wallop with the butt of a rifle – provided someone did not get there first with the point of a bayonet...

CHAPTER 11 – [1916]

Brigade Headquarters

20th January 1916 – still at the front line, my company was eagerly waiting to be relieved. Sheltering under my groundsheet with my Morse code transmitter carefully protected, I was prepared to accept further instructions.

It turned out to be my lucky day. The codeword "HORSE" came through – which was the code for my Company. The message was to the effect that a shorthand-typist was required at Brigade Headquarters! I was more than excited and so as soon as I had completed the message I bustled my way along the trench until I found my Captain.

"That's me, sir! That's me, sir!" I stammered, excitedly. When I had calmed down a little, he read the message and queried my abilities before consulting the CO. And so it was that I was instructed to send a message to Brigade Headquarters saying that a suitable applicant was 'on his way', I then hastily made my way down the communi-cation trenches in a state of great excitement.

In Mazingarbe, I located the Brigade Headquarters where the Quartermaster Sergeant (QMS) took me to see the Staff Captain. He was as friendly as his rank would allow and I was immediately taken to be paraded before the General.

I stood rigidly to "attention", but was soon told to "stand easy". After eyeing me from head to toe, the General said to the Captain, "See that this man gets clean clothing and a good feed."

Later on, feeling, and no doubt looking, more like a soldier, I was beckoned to sit down at an improvised table, illuminated by a candle placed at each side of an Oliver typewriter.

Having passed my typing test, I was advised to produce a Shorthand Typing Certificate which would entitle me to extra pay. I wrote to my Mother asking her to forward my certificates. However, when these eventually came, they were sent straight back to a Paymaster in England! Weeks afterwards, they were returned, along with a letter which rejected my claim, stating that someone on our staff was already drawing 'proficiency pay'. It turned out to be the QMS, who was, incidentally, not a Scot. He was a very learned type and had never done any real soldiering. Nevertheless, he held a high NCO rank and was paid for doing the same work as myself.

Our headquarters were slightly below ground level, cave-like and candlelit throughout, where, as well as myself and a Quartermaster Sergeant, there were also the Brigadier General, Brigade Major, Staff Captain and the Intelligence Officer.

I had to tackle my work on a table which I shared with Lieutenant Georgeson (the Intelligence Officer), but most after small table top was commandeered by him as he endeavoured to solve the problem of joining several aerial photographs together in order to arrive at a continuous picture of the trenches confronting our Sector. This task was not easily achieved, because there were approximately twenty 10 x 8 inch stills in glossy black and white.

The photography was excellent, and the details of the observation posts, wire defences, firing lines and communication trenches were outstandingly clear.

Our pilots and aerial photographers had to be admired for the risks they must have been taken in flying so low in order to procure such valuable information.

My new 'niche' in Mazingarbe was more than I could have dreamt of after roughing it for so long in the vicinity of "No Man's Land". Having known what it was like to sleep hunched up in an open trench in all weathers, I considered it a great luxury to be able to stretch out on a dry floor – and what a treat it was to get hot food every day!

❖ ❖ ❖

25th January – Burns Night. No haggis! And as the village had been razed flat way back in September, the only 'hard stuff' we could get hold of, had come from the Germans. I was just getting used to my new environment when we moved to Noeux Les Mines. Since our arrival in France – only six months ago – we had been given no leave. By virtue of my position, I became aware that arrangements were being made for a limited number of men from each of the battalions in the Brigade to be given leave. Armed with this knowledge, I put in a request and was granted permission to join the others in the Camerons' allocation. What a thrill it would be to get away from the Front for a while!

I left Noeux Les Mines on the 29th January and as a result of the well-organised arrangements by the RTOs I reached home on the 31st January at 9am, giving my mother a real surprise. I was just too late to see my little brother before he left for school. No time was lost in providing me with the best breakfast I had eaten for months.

Keeping up the tradition of the "Shiny Seventh" by well-grooming myself in double-quick time (always a pleasure this) I cock-a-hooped it through the village to the little school where I had learned my ABCs. Peeping through the classroom door I could see my (old) Headmaster and had no difficulty in pin-pointing my brother who was in the 'junior standard'.

I wasted no time in knocking on the glass door and was immediately invited in, and taken by the hand to the middle of the large classroom, where I stood facing the pupils of the four 'standards'. I had taken with me a German helmet as a souvenir and when this was placed on the head of a little boy in the front row he completely 'lost his head' much to the amusement of the other children.

There was a considerable amount of whispering and the Head turned to the children and asked if it was a holiday they wanted. The answer, accompanied by cheers, was unanimous. Before the day was out most of the villagers were aware that I, the first one in the village to enlist, was back from the Front. Their 'wanting to know everything' curiosity could be well appreciated.

7th February – After only nine days on leave I joined the troop train at Victoria and had an uneventful return to the Philosophe Headquarters. There I remained until the 18th March and during that time there were many 'take-overs' involving all units of the Brigade plus the Kings Own Scottish Borderers, Highland Light Infantry and the Inniskillings. We went back to Allouagne once more for a breather.

28th March – This day was the culmination of some hectic organisation behind the Lines. Each Commanding Officer carried out an inspection of his Unit, after which the whole Brigade marched past the General Officer Commanding the 1st Army. For all ranks, it was the highlight of their life when they were presented with well-merited medals.

This break from the Front line enabled our 15th Scottish Division to undergo various exercises including the use of smoke-screens.

10th April – It was a surprise to learn that Lt. Col. Sandilands was relinquishing command of the Camerons. On the 13th a 'farewell' gathering took place and it was most pleasing to see the people of Allouagne lining the streets. A few days after this event the General Officer Commanding of our Division carried out another inspection prior to our going up Front again. Since being relieved by the Highland Light Infantry in the Hulluch Sector on the 20th March the Camerons have had a peaceful time in Allouagne.

24th April – Now under the command of Major Cunningham, the Camerons went into the line at the Quarries Section, where the situation was hotting up. They relieved the Royal Sussex Regiment and had to contend with gas, shelling and mines being exploded.

30th April – The 10th Gordon Highlanders took over from the Camerons, whose turn it was now to go into Reserve at Noyelles. There I had the chance to get all the news from my pals whom I forsook hurriedly to go on to Brigade Headquarters.

4th May – Not much rest as the Camerons went back and relieved the Gordons. This was a very lively day and night, with bombardments from both sides and to add to the chaos the Royal Engineers exploded mines at the Hairpin. Within seconds the Camerons rushed forward and took up positions on the far side of these. They were subjected to heavy shelling for a long period whilst holding these craters and unfortunately suffered some casualties.

8th May – Another change, Major Cunningham who had been in charge since Colonel Sandilands left, handed over command to Major Marsh of the King's Own Scottish Borderers.

The Royal Engineers were tunnelling non-stop and like other units in the Brigade the Camerons were fully employed carrying sacks of earth away.

19th May – This time the King's Own Scottish Borderers came and took over from the Camerons who via La Bourse and Noyelles went into the Hohenzollern Redoubt and relieved the Argyll & Sutherland Highlanders.

23rd May – Almost daily, little mines were being exploded, but early on this beautiful spring morning a whopper was sent up – by the enemy, we understood.

24th May – There was quite a bit of aerial activity foreboding that action would be taking place soon. A Fokker was brought down. The pilot (who turned out to be a German Prince) and his Observer were found to be dead. As the plane had fallen behind our lines there was a rush towards it. The Prince had been wearing an artificial leg which had become separated from his body and 'chips' of this together with other little items were soon taken as souvenirs.

Rumours were rife that Kitchener had made arrangements for the Russians to land in the North of Scotland, make their way through England and cross over to France to support us! This was cheerful news, but alas, despite persistent enquiries there was no evidence of it happening. Then came the blow. On the 5th June, HMS *Hampshire* was torpedoed and Kitchener was lost. What were we going do without the General? Could we still win? Such were the thoughts of we young soldiers. We had it drilled into us once again – "DON'T LISTEN TO RUMOURS".

We found ourselves back in Bethune – the last time we had been here the Camerons Pipe Band gave a display in the centre of town. I was fortunate enough to be billeted in a hotel which had been commandeered earlier whereas some of the other Camerons had to be content with occupying a tobacco factory.

There was a considerable amount of interchanging between the units in the Brigade. The Camerons went into support in the Hulluch Sector to relieve the Royal Scottish Fusiliers. The Lancaster Regiment joined them for breaking-in purposes, as did the East Surreys a week later.

21st June – Our planes attacked and brought down six hostile balloons in flames. Success, however little, was always cheerful news. Soon after this, seeking revenge, enemy planes were seen hovering around and a real aerial battle commenced immediately above our Headquarters. However, due to the evasive action is taken by the pilots, the aircraft soon moved away, but remained visible for some time.

For about twenty five minutes five of our planes were fighting it out against six of the enemy's. It was a thrilling dog-fight until the German machines withdrew, some losing height rapidly. Unfortunately two of our planes came down within our lines and it was found that the pilot in each was dead.

28th June – A night raid was made by the Camerons but they did not succeed in bringing back any prisoners. The failure was attributed to the fact that the earlier bombardment by our artillery had not demolished the wire protecting enemy trenches, rendering it impossible for them to carry out their mission.

Judging by the lack of immediate return fire it was possible that the use of gas had been partially effective, but nevertheless it would have been sheer madness to attempt crawling through the barbed wire.

It was a precarious withdrawal because dozens of Verey Lights (parachute flares) almost turned night into day, forcing our men to 'keep down' or crawl into shell-holes to avoid being spotted. Whilst this was going on, the men in the firing line were more than ever on the *qui vive*, ready to join in or give a hand with the enemy prisoners, who we anticipated would be brought in. Irrespective of the outcome of the raid, the Camerons were due to be relieved and were certainly glad to get back into billets at and around Bethune. A and German aircraft, a Taube, had the audacity to come over in broad daylight and drop a bomb just a hundred yards from our Headquarters. As a precaution against a second bomb, our scheduled movements were temporarily restricted, but the lone marauder did not return to his base – two of 'our' aircraft saw to that.

A despatch rider of the 46th Brigade who had called on us had the misfortune to be run over by a lorry and instantly killed.

The swimming pool at the Ecole des Jeunes Filles was placed at our disposal and the organised sessions were much appreciated – despite the absence of the 'jeunes filles' (young ladies).

6th July – We left Bethune for the Hohenzollern Section. The Camerons took over from the Royal Scottish Fusiliers and four days later were relieved by the 8th Seaforths.

14th July – The Camerons replaced the Black Watch. For the past four weeks the Brigade had been alternating between the Firing Line and Support trenches and it was a very costly period. There were gas attacks and mines were exploding in No Man's Land to the accompaniment of heavy bombardments, supplemented to a lesser degree by rifle grenades – all of which intensified the "we won't give in" attitude. The result of this cataclysm was that our trenches were severely damaged over a wide area and constant repairs were necessary despite the difficulties caused by intermittent shelling.

17th July – Following an extremely heavy bombardment, the Germans made a night raid on our trenches. Apart from a few killed and wounded the Camerons had some 'missing' – probably taken prisoner – which of course was the sole purpose of the raid.

22nd July – The Royal Berkshire Regiment relieved the Camerons who went to Houchin.

The whole Brigade was now on the move, marching through Dieval, Averdoingt, Occoches, Autheux, Fienvillers, Maouts, Talmas and Mirvaux. We realised that we must be going to another part of the Front. During the long trek, where no billets were available, we had bivouacs, so it was not a 'rough time' exercise.

Onward, ever onward through La Houssoye until we pulled up at Albert – just two years after the outbreak of war.

Each day we started off at dawn in order to miss the discomfort of the afternoon's heat and this meant arriving early at our billets, thereby giving plenty of time for whatever recreation we desired. There was usually a little 'attraction' in some of the villages we passed through in the early stages, but our greatest pleasure of all was finding a stream where we could enjoy a swim.

With ample time at our disposal in the evening, football was the favourite pastime and what better exercise? On the way south there was always the dreaded menace of enemy planes, though mostly these were only taking photographs so their presence did not seriously threaten us.

As we approached Albert we could see the Basilique. At the top, over the front entrance, silhouetted against the sky was a statue of the Virgin Mary and Child. The nearer we got, the clearer the details became. The figure was leaning forward with the child in her outstretched arms in such a manner as to suggest that She was saying, "Save Him, Save Him".

Every soldier who fought on the Somme always wanted to know 'if the Virgin had fallen' – because it had become a superstition (I don't know how it started) that when the Virgin fell, it would signal the end of the German Empire.

Basilique Notre-Dame de Brebieres - Albert 1916. Soldiers believed that when the statue of the Madonna fell from the spire, the German Empire would fall and the war would be over.

CHAPTER 12 – [1916]

The Battle of the Somme

It was ghastly to see a shell explode near a convoy and actually witness horses, guns and ammunition wagons blown up. In addition to restricting progress it was unsightly to see some of the earlier casualties stacked up at the side of the roads.

The nearer we went towards the battle area, the greater was the evidence of the strafing prior to the commencement of this new action. The Battle of the Somme was already raging, but the Brigade was still a good way behind the Front Line – in Divisional Reserve.

It came as a surprise when two of us were given most of the day off. We hitched-hiked it to Amiens (42 km away) to see the wonderful Cathedral. How peaceful it was at Mass, but as soon as we came out of the cathedral, the sound of distant gunfire was a chilling reminder of what we had to go back to.

9th August – The first rainfall for three weeks. Exceptionally heavy gunfire. The Australians attacked during the night and captured more than 70 Germans, exceeding all expectations.

Although elated at meeting up with the Aussies, our lads could not understand how it was that they were getting four shillings a day pay whereas we British got only one shilling – less if we were 'making an allocation' for some are paid to be sent to our families at home.

14th August – The Brigade, which had been in Reserve, now left Albert for Contalmaison – conspicuous on a hilltop, or rather what was left of it as a result of the bombing before being captured by our troops on the 10th July 1916.

The downpour had not abated and it was sometime before we could find a suitable site. Eventually we came across an exceptionally deep dugout which had been made and occupied by the Germans. The layout seemed to indicate that it had accommodated six officers and staff, with plaques fixed on the walls indicating various 'departments'.

Whilst in Reserve there were many positional changes and all the Units had been providing Working Parties.

17th August – The Brigade was engaged in a major attack at Switch Elbow. The Camerons achieved their objective, but depleted by heavy casualties they had to yield ground. The Gordons brought up more ammunition and with the assistance of the Seaforths the counter-attack was successful. The Germans attacked the Brigade on our right and whilst this was happening the Camerons and Black Watch re-took the Switch Elbow. Our casualties were heavy, but the number of Germans captured exceeded our losses. After this, the Camerons were relieved by the Seaforths and went back into Reserve.

18th August – In the afternoon we discharged a smoke screen. The Germans launched an attack but were repulsed.

To intensify the struggle on this particular day, the Australians on our left captured 300 yards of heavily fortified trenches. "One of ours" had a high old time with an enemy fighter which went down in flames.

19th August – Not far from us was Becourt Wood and this was given a real battering by the Germans.

20th August – Contalmaison was once again subjected to concentrated shellfire and our own battery positions there had a rough time through the night. Although sprinkled with gas shells there were no casualties – thanks to the efficiency of our respirators. I got a slight sniff of this: it had a sickly sweet smell but I suffered no ill effects. With gas shells still coming over, the Camerons, despite their mauling three days ago, had pulled themselves together and were sent in to replace the Gordons.

21st August – The Germans seemingly had something up their sleeves, for during the night we had to contend with a prolonged gas attack.

22nd August – The Gordons in the Front Line were relieved by the Camerons who commenced, without delay, to construct strong points which they completed and occupied during the night – but not without a few casualties.

24th August – The switching round of the Black Watch and the Gordons resulted in the Camerons going back to Reserve before going to Contalmaison.

26th August – One of our own planes, flying low behind our lines, suddenly made a downward dive and crashed. It was thought that it had been struck by one of our shells 'going over'. Unfortunately the pilot was dead, the observer dying on the spot shortly afterwards. This mishap took place just before other planes crossed into enemy territory.

29th August – Two of our Observation Balloons were struck by lightning and came down out of sight. It was a peaceful day if one ignored the violent thunderstorm and the exceptionally heavy rain.

30th August – The Northumberland Fusiliers relieved the Camerons who went into Divisional Reserve.

31st August – Just after we left Contalmaison yesterday there was a surrender: 2 Sergeant Majors and 40 other ranks, accompanied by 2 German Officers came over our lines. Apart from the Battle of Loos last September we were now experiencing the hottest fighting since our arrival in France, with action taking place not only on our immediate front but also on both flanks.

4th September – For the past few days we have had reasonably fine weather and astonishingly, very little trouble from the other side, the latter foreboding something big on its way?

5th September – Major Beck leaves the Brigade and Captain Barge replaces him. We strike our mobile headquarters at Albert and move on to Memetz Wood. Reconnoitring through and around the Wood it was very evident that our artillery had given it a severe pounding, as the shell-holes were many and deep. Scattered about, there were German wagons, gun carriages and immense quantities of ammunition of various types. In addition, it seemed as if an ammunition dump had been blown sky-high during our preliminary bombardments.

One German plane zoomed into Shelter Wood. The Camerons went into the Front Line again and relieved the Highland Light Infantry.

6/7th September – Throughout the night there was unusual air activity by our planes. Another enemy plane brought down by our gunfire just after daybreak.

On this night there was a heavy bombardment by the Germans on our left which resulted in Shelter Wood getting the brunt of this.

The Camerons, who were in the old German line were once again relieved by the Seaforths.

It was another day of intense aerial activity by both sides and in a dog fight we brought down five small planes without our sustaining any casualties.

8th September – Still another bombardment, this time by us. It started at noon and did not let up till 5.30pm.

The 9th Black Watch of our 15th Scottish Division had the 1st Division on its immediate right and jointly they attacked the north-west corner of High Wood at 6pm – only half an hour after the lifting of the blitz. A remarkable liaison.

At 6.15pm the Black Watch with the Gloucesters on their right, took the German trench – but it was empty except for a few German casualties.

At 8pm the Gloucesters were withdrawn leaving the Black Watch with both flanks exposed. The Germans attempted to surround them, but the Highlanders, after repulsing the enemy returned to their original jumping-off position.

9th September – Another assault on High Wood was made today by units of our Division but our own 44th Brigade was not involved. Unsuccessful.

10th September – We left our headquarters at Memetz Wood and established others at Shelter Wood. Companies from the 149th and 159th Brigades relieved our 44th Brigade.

11th September – The Camerons went into the Front Line and took over from the Gordons.

13th September – After only three days at Shelter Wood we left for Albert and despite further damage to the Basilique the Virgin Mary was still 'hanging' there although in a different position. The town was scarcely recognisable.

En route we witnessed another aerial dog-fight, our planes bringing down a German fighter in flames. It landed somewhere between the firing line and Contalmaison. The Royal Scottish Fusiliers relieved the Camerons who went back to rest near Albert which was always liable to receive further packets.

14th September – Not much respite, as we left Albert once again for Shelter Wood. The hasty return certainly foreshadowed something urgent and unexpected, as indeed there was.

At 6.30am the Division attacked and captured Martinpuich. By 7.25am we had taken 300 prisoners and driven beyond Martinpuich into enemy territory. The Canadians on the left were holding half of Courcelette.

From where I stood on the outskirts to the left of the village I could see some-strange looking objects – like miniature steam road-rollers. This is a date I always remember – 15th September 1916.

It was strange to see these weird machines crawling forward with infantry, bayonets fixed, cautiously advancing behind them. It was also heart-warming to see the Germans on the run.

Alas! There were some that did not move – possibly due to mechanical faults or tilting over in trenches or muddy craters. It was almost impossible to restrain men from leaving their posts in order to satisfy their curiosity. What were these strange contrivances? No one could give them a name at that time but later they become known as 'tanks'. Why were there not more of them? If there had been, their employment might have been the means of shortening the war. As it was, they were a distinct boost to general morale, and the story went around that "Lloyd George was reported to have announced that if these are successful we shall order more and more and more". Too late. The Germans adopted our idea without wasting time – as we were to learn later to our regret...

The whole of Courcelette was taken and many prisoners were escorted into hurriedly constructed 'cages' just a few hundred yards from our Headquarters. There was much elation and excitement all round at the spectacle of so many Germans being marched away with their hands above their heads. In fact the prisoners did not seem the least bit downhearted – they were probably thankful that their fighting days were over.

Somehow I managed to convey to one of the German Officers that I would like his button-like cap badge as a souvenir, but in view of his surprisingly polite retort "please wait until the war is over," I saw no reason for persuasion, as there were sure to be others.

As I and a handful of others were interestedly looking at the prisoners, an NCO (not a kilted one) came over and shouted – vociferously – "What the **** are you doing here? You came up to do your little bit but it is a damned little bit you do! Get up into the Front Line and bring back your own prisoners!"

Our 'Liquid Fire' had evidently done its work. It was shocking to see the effect of this weapon on human beings for some of those whom we had just captured were physically incapable of putting their hands up when being marched off.

17th September – Brigade left Shelter Wood for Villa Wood.

18th September – Villa Wood to Albert.

19th September – From Albert to Lavieville. The Camerons were relieved by the 8th Yorkshire Regiment and went to billets at Franvillers.

20th September – From Lavieville we moved our Headquarters from Fransvillers (12 km) so the whole Brigade has now been virtually reassembled.

25th September – First anniversary of the Battle of Loos. (How many of us remain?) My war-torn kilt is replaced – what a coincidence. There are mild rumblings in the distance but we consider we are fortunate in having such a pleasant location for a much needed break. Silence is broken by fifteen German planes passing over the village. It was reported later in the day that they had dropped a number of bombs on Amiens.

26th September – Breathing space. A few of us had a trek to Amiens and were pleased to see that the bombs dropped yesterday did not affect the centre of town. In the very large Cathedral, a service was taking place for two French soldiers, each of the bulky coffins being draped with the now familiar flag – *bleu-blanc-rouge* – covered with wreaths and sprinkled with holy water by a priest. The mourners, of whom there were many, included *poilus* (French soldiers) and civilian dignitaries.

28th September – We 'found' some bikes and cycled in Heilly and on to Mericourt where we visited Prisoner of War Camp No. 2.

1st October – Making the best of 'play-time' we cycled to Behencourt.

6th October – We were looking forward to Brigade Sports planned for today but unfortunately these had to be cancelled on instructions to 'move up'.

We packed up at Franvillers and went to Becourt Wood where we had to be satisfied with tents for our Head-quarters – no protection whatsoever should anything come over.

Here I came across a school chum, Johnny Denovan, a smart young officer in the 10th Scottish Rifles. Although still in the rear, the Brigade did suffer casualties from the frequent shelling. Temporary trenches did not offer much protection and it is interesting to note that the Camerons occupied some which actually had been, hurriedly no doubt, made into a cemetery.

8th October – We leave Becourt Wood for Martinpuich. The approaches to Martinpuich were being heavily shelled and we were obliged to take cover for some time. This village had previously undergone quite a strafing and when we eventually reached it we had no alternative but to 'lie low' once again. (I suppose our use of the word 'strafe' came from seeing signs bearing the message "Gott Strafe England" [God punish England] which we would find in almost every village from which the Huns had been dislodged.)

I pitied the poor cook and the horses – for there was no water here. The nearest supply was about a mile away.

11th October – Heavy shelling for the past three days. Johnny Oliphant, one of the staff, wounded on his way to Signals. The Gordons were relieved by the Camerons in the Front Line but not without casualties.

12th October – We put up a smoke screen – quite spectacular. The South Africans (9th Div.) on the right of our Brigade launched an attack but had to withdraw from their objective – The Dump – West of Butte de Warlencourt.

13th October – Martinpuich heavily shelled most of the day. During relief by the 8th Seaforths both battalions sustained casualties.

14th October – The 12th Highland Light Infantry once again relieved the Camerons. As shelling had eased considerably we had a stroll round the village and from what we saw it was evident that the villagers had not expected to vacate their houses hurriedly. Nevertheless, this must have happened, judging by the amount of goods and chattels abandoned in their normal positions. The village had previously been taken by the 45th and 46th Brigades whilst we were in Reserve.

15th October – We moved our Headquarters to Villa Wood and en route our trucks were damaged by shellfire from which we were taking cover.

19th October – Left Villa Wood and settled down (for how long?) at a spot between Becourt Hill and La Boiselle. The Camerons moved up to relieve the Black Watch – just the reverse of what happened on the 24th August.

21st October – I went to Amiens with a despatch from the Brigade Major.

23rd October – The Black Watch (in reciprocation) relieved the Camerons who went back into support.

24th October – Quickly relieved by the Highland Light Infantry the Camerons when back into reserve.

25th October – Some of us explored a mine shaft leading to a crater. This was just like a coal mine. There was a miniature railway for bringing back the excavations. Apparently this was the biggest mine shaft ever constructed by the Royal Engineers, it having taken several months to complete. This was subsequently exploded in front of the German firing line south of La Boiselle.

27th October – Still well back, the Camerons relieved the Scottish Rifles.

LEAVE! The SDR dug me out at 10pm and I was completely surprised when he handed me a pass for Blighty! I hastily left with the minimum pack and passed the rest of the night/early morning at Albert.

28th October – Turned my back on Albert once more and hitch-hiked to Amiens in time for the 5.40pm train.

29th October – After a comfortable night's ride I arrived at Rouen at 4am. The Railway Transport Officer had been most helpful in that I was allowed to get on an ordinary passenger train instead of one of the special 'troop' trains which was due some time later. This was a treat despite being crammed with civilians and Froggies, all of whom were very friendly and keen to learn of my exploits in the Front Line. All I dared say was *"No comprong"*. I left the station café at 9am and made my way to the Reinforcement Camp. There was no prospects of getting a train from Rouen or a boat from Le Havre so was obliged to remain at the camp.

5th November – After one week at the Camp I left Rouen at 4.30pm and arrived at Le Havre at 9.05pm.

6th November – Spent a comfortable night on board the troopship with couldn't-be-better camaraderie. We did not sail until the evening – a long wait when one is itching to get back home.

7th November – I arrived at Southampton at 9.30am and reached Waterloo just after noon. When we (a sergeant was with me) got outside Waterloo Station we were 'lost' in the Big City.

I asked the driver of a one-horse railway delivery van which was stationery at the kerbside how to get to Shaftesbury Hotel just off Shaftesbury Avenue. He said 'jump on' and pulling ourselves up by the thick rope at the rear – our swinging kilts amusing onlookers – we were duly deposited at the hotel in St Martin's Lane half-an-hour or so later. My uncle (the owner) was speaking to the uniformed doorman when we were 'unloaded' and the driver was duly rewarded in English money instead of our bits and pieces of French francs.

My uncle quickly observed that I had no greatcoat on this cold wintry day and it was not long before he took me out and bought a trench coat 'to cover my knees'. He asked me how much pay I was receiving and when I surprised him by saying that as a mere Private I had sixpence per day (I started off with the usual one shilling per day, but having no need for all that money in the trenches I allocated half of it to my Mother), he made sure that I would have whatever I wanted during my leave – in addition to some "readies".

Imagine leaving the battle front to stay in London's most recently-constructed West End Hotel! We certainly were feted there. We did a lot of sight-seeing, but so did others – especially when we climbed the rear winding exterior steps of an open-decked bus. We wondered why so many people were peering up at us!

Now well-fed, clothed and with plenty of money I left Euston at 11.30pm.

8th November – I arrived at Glasgow Central – too early to get the first train towards my home in Eaglesham. Sharing the compartment on my way North was a friendly gentleman who offered me a drink out of his pocket flask which I gladly accepted. He said that he was the manager of Glasgow Celtic Football Club and promised to entertain me 'when I go out' and even to give me a trial if the game appealed to me. When I got as far as the train would carry me I completed the remaining four miles on a char-a-banc which had a huge gas-filled bag fitted to the roof. I arrived home at 11.30am – twelve days after starting out.

12th November – My 21st birthday and I am given a gold ring by my Mother – my Father being in the army in Ireland.

14th November – After only six days at home I leave Glasgow at 10.20pm for London.

15th November – Arrived Euston at 9am and stayed overnight at the Shaftesbury Hotel where once again I was admirably regaled.

16th November – Left Waterloo Station for Southampton. Embarked on the SS *Donegal* at 7pm but the weather was too stormy to attempt a Channel crossing, so we remained overnight in the Solent.

17th November – After twelve hours delay we sailed down Southampton Water at 9pm.

18th November – It was a rough passage. On deck the cold wind was really blowing, hence the accommodation in the converted lounge left very little space for stretching out. No one was sorry when we berthed at Le Havre at 8am. We reported to the Rest Camp where we stayed until 9pm then left for a train due to leave at 10pm. Travel weary I had a good nap on the train.

19th November – Reached Rouen at 9.30am and had ample time to explore and visit cafés until boarding a train at 1.30pm. This did not leave until 2.10pm and it was 10.30pm before we arrived at Romney's Camp Blaincourt. There the train was divided up for other destinations.

20th November – On 'coming-to' early in the morning I found we have not moved from the station. It seemed to be an important junction for there were several trains waiting along side in which were French and Belgium soldiers and sailors. There was the usual souvenir-swapping: fags, badges, buttons, bully beef, Macconnochi rations, condensed milk etc. We did not leave this junction until 2.40pm.

21st November – What a slow journey – not reaching Frechencourt until 2.15am. This is the Divisional railhead. I was on my own and walked till dawn, slowly of course, and was relieved when I got a lift in a truck which was going to Bresle. It was there I re-joined our Headquarters. As I went on leave on the 27th October and our Corps had gone into Reserve on the 3rd November – that was whilst I was away – little wonder I had such difficulty in locating our Headquarters. This is the first day I have really felt homesick. Fortunately this state of mind soon vanished when I heard that Brigade Sports were to be held later in the day.

Blessed by suitable weather it was a real spectacle watching the kilt-swinging competitors being urged to victory by such a mass of men whose thoughts were being diverted from what they had been through.

The Camerons had the highest number of points and won the Silver Bugle presented by General W.G. Wilkinson, CB, MVO. The Seaforths were second, the Black Watch and Gordons sharing third place. This Cameron victory was a good tonic.

26th November – Still in Corps Reserve. The General Officer Commanding 15th Division carried out an inspection. Weather-wise we could not have had a worse day for having to stand like 'stookies'.

The only bit of excitement was a concerted effort to extinguish a fire which had broken out in the Camp of the Seaforths.

Bresle was undoubtedly a convenient location to hold an inspection. I was on leave when the Corps Commander gave us the 'once over' but was present when Sir Douglas Haig, our Commander-in-Chief, reviewed us.

29th November – On this cold but dry day a horse-race meeting took place and it was pleasing to see our Brigade win the 'big un' – the Martinpuich Plate.

30th November – St. Andrew's Day. This four-week away-from-it-all break with just enough exercise to keep us fit was much appreciated but it had to come to an end and we moved forward to Albert via Lavieville and Millencourt. Despite bombardments over these recent months causing further damage to the Basilique, the statue of the Virgin Mary was still there. Each time we came back to this area we found that the position of the statue had changed and it was now hanging almost upside-down. We were anxiously waiting for it to come right down – thus indicating the fall of the German Empire.

One of my most frightening experiences was on the Somme. Movements of guns, ammunition, supplies and troops towards the Front took place in darkness and as I had seen from the aerial photographs, the roads were very limited in number and hardly appeared suitable for such heavy traffic. Going up one night and nearing the Front Line, for a long time there was scarcely any movement in either direction. By the brilliance of the never-ending umbrella of Verey Lights, supplemented by the flashes of the heavies, the agonising chaos was vividly illuminated. Add to this the maddening noises made by the frightened mules being handled by the Gurkhas. The enemy shelling of our supply route was the worst I had ever experienced and with the ever-increasing shrapnel bursts all around the obvious thing was to take cover, and this I did by hastily throwing myself into a roadside gully.

There seemed no end to this now ferocious bombardment and as I remained down there crouched in the mud, I could not see what was happening immediately above me. Suddenly, a mule laden with machine guns and ammunition fell into the shallow trench nearby. It landed on its back about six feet away from me and the trench being so narrow the frightened animal, its four legs very active, could not right itself despite the frantic efforts of the muleteers. I didn't understand 'horse language' but was certainly relieved when the animal received the *coup de grace* from a sorrowful Gurkha. To be kicked to death by a mule was not a pleasant prospect.

Not until dawn did this hell ease up. It was only then that the sickening sight of such carnage of men and beasts made me realise how lucky, or unlucky, one can be. I shall not readily forget the saddened faces of some of these small thick-set soldiers as they surveyed the now dead or dying animals that had been transported with them all the way from Nepal. They struggled to salvage the equipment and weapons by transferring them from the backs of the dead animals to those of the survivors, although these were, seemingly, already overloaded. It really was a surprise to see these miniature soldiers carrying such heavy loads.

7th December – Albert by this time was now almost a shambles – not a complete house could be seen and groups of men busy clearing the streets to facilitate movement of supplies and troops.

11th December – Visited Amiens once more to see a bit of life. When out drinking in the cafes, Grenadine was no longer my drink of choice; rum was more in keeping with my current circumstances and experience.

16th December – With the Virgin Mary still clasping the Child, we left Albert to go into huts at Shelter Wood as Divisional Reserve.

19th December – Leaving Shelter Wood we made our way up towards Martinpuich, stopping on top of a ridge for I do not know how long as a fierce battle was raging straight ahead.

Someone said to me "You'll get your head wet – look at your helmet". I took it off, examined it and found a gash about two inches long right on the crown. On reflection I remembered getting a 'ping' and having to readjust my tin hat but thought nothing of it at the time thinking that a piece of flying earth had struck it. Another lucky escape!

We were high up and it was a clear day, and within my view was the biggest mass of troops I had ever seen. Still more troops were moving slowly up from the rear. Our numbers were swelling gradually, but the only movement detectable in the immediate vicinity was that of men trying to keep warm from the biting wind.

CHAPTER 13 – [1916/1917]

Hors de Combat

19ᵗʰ December – On the ridge where we were halted, a metre-gauge train – similar to the type used in coal mines – loaded with ammunition for the gun-pits ahead had become derailed. There was no shortage of manpower and the little bogie train was soon successfully restored to its proper position. This little bit of diversion took place amidst intermittent shrapnel bursts when we should normally be taking cover instead of exposing ourselves. If only one shell had made a direct hit on that train I shudder to think how many lives would have been lost.

Whatever happened after that I do not know except that I remember being put on a stretcher and seeing others on the ground beside me.

I was carried to an RAMC ambulance (horse-drawn) which was on the roadway nearby. I was manoeuvred into the bottom left-hand berth, feet first and sometime later I felt something wet on my legs.

It was a rough passage, undoubtedly due to the many potholes and the stop-go jerky ride was made more frightening by many shell bursts. I pitied the driver and the two horses.

There was a deafening explosion. The ambulance shook and rested almost completely on its left side. It must have been with extreme difficulty that we wounded were extricated.

The ambulance was badly damaged and the poor horses were either dead, injured or entangled in the traces. Fortunately this happened not far from a Dressing Station at Becourt and we were carried there on the stretchers – past two dead horses.

According to an Orderly's first comment, I must have had a packet, but happily from my point of view it turned out that the blood on my legs was from the chap who was above me in the ambulance.

However, after a first-aid cleaning I was transferred to a Casualty Clearance Station. This was housed in a large marquee. I was at the head of the queue, impatiently waiting my turn to be put on the table, and as I lay there I could see some poor chap's leg fixed to a pulley, with surgeons in attendance. I must have groaned or coughed, at any rate made a noise and the orderlies were instructed to "take that man away". I remember being put on the table but not being taken off it. On 'coming to' I put my hand down and was overjoyed to find that my leg was still there!

22nd December – Three days after being wounded I left the C.C.S. at 5pm.

23rd December – I was admitted to Boulougne Hospital at 6.25am. After an early examination it was a great relief to be told that it had been decided not to amputate – here.

24th December – I felt greatly encouraged watching others, despite sticks, crutches or wheelchairs, making bold efforts to assist in decorating the Ward for Christmas.

25th December – In the very early hours of Christmas Day, Father Christmas (one of the sisters) crept along the Ward pinning Xmas Pillows to the bottom end of the beds. Seeing that I spotted her and had the audacity to give her a naughty wink, she popped in a few more cigarettes. In the afternoon a different Father Xmas came round and personally distributed gifts. Mine? A leather case containing a steel mirror, size three by four inches. Altogether a happy day and a real joy to chat with so many civilians.

26th December – As a temporary measure I had splints fitted to keep me going until I got to Dear Old Blighty. The Christmas festivities over, what next to pass away the time? Well, my bed was right at the end of a long ward adjoining the ablutions. The traffic was never ending. I took my writing block and pencil and when anyone went in with his bottle I asked his name. On his coming out I asked him to tell me how many fluid ounces he had disposed of! This went on for about an hour until Matron came over to my bed.

Querying my self-appointment as a fact finder I explained that I was only trying to kill time and keep my brain in working order. "Well, you certainly seem to be good at figures!" was all she said. After lunch a Sister, cheerfully smiling approached with an armful of books which she slowly placed in front of me. I was even more bewildered when she said "I believe you are very good with figures". My reward for being so clever was that I was given the job of working out the cost of the ward's food bill by adding up the columns in a large book. There were pages and pages of different items and their respective prices. Strangely enough, I thoroughly enjoyed this diversion which occupied a few hours on each of three days.

I was fortunate in still having my diary, certain items in which were noted in shorthand. With nothing else to do I checked up on the towns, villages and hamlets I had passed through and wondered what had happened to the civilians I had met. The very mention of these evoked memories of some sad experiences. Perhaps they no longer exist but I have listed them in Chapter 19 as there is the possibility that one day I may be in a position to re-visit the battle areas.

4th January 1917 – It was decided that nothing more could be done for me here so was taken to Boulogne Station.

5th January – I arrived at Le Harve in the early hours of the morning but it was daylight before I was stretchered on to HM Hospital Ship *Carisbrook Castle*. It was pitiful to see so many walking, hobbling and stretcher cases, although every one of them was being carefully handled.

Just as I was comfortably installed below decks I noticed the time was 9.40am and peering through a porthole I could see the French coast receding. I recollect murmuring "I hope I never have to come back here again..."

As I lay there under the protection of the Red Cross my thoughts were of those I had left behind – not only to combat the Boche – but to survive the horrible conditions in the trenches at this time of year. I well remember one occasion when a rather young Chaplain was threading his way along our front line trench. It was encouraging to chat with him but the whistling of shells etc. interrupted our conversation. I don't think he relished his first visit to the Firing Line, but at least he came to appreciate the almost intolerable conditions and hardships which the frontline soldiers had to withstand. The Chaplains were frequently conspicuous by their absence in the frontline, and were usually to the found well behind the lines. It was very touching, however, when on one occasion the entire battalion formed up to pay their last respects to one of our fallen comrades. The improvised catafalque and coffin were covered with a Union Jack. The service took place to the undesirable accompaniment of gunfire and ended with the lament of a piper. That was the one and only funeral service I saw on the battlefield.

My reminiscences also include those not in military uniform who too were fighting this awful war – the Salvation Army for instance. For this Corps I had the greatest admiration and always shall. Within earshot and range of the enemy guns I was surprised to see a flag of the Salvation Army fluttering over a camouflaged hut. Inside there was a sprinkling of all ranks, from various units, some of whom were suffering from minor injuries whilst others were sprawled on the floor or enjoying a hot drink. It was evident that all were being cared for – voluntarily.

I, like many others, was temporarily incapable of completing a free-issue 'field postcard' but one kind-hearted 'Sally Army' member who was busying himself with a likewise handicapped man came to my aid. The printed matter on these cards was very brief and to the point so it was a question of striking out the items inapplicable to the situation and signing it or getting someone else to do it for you.

Well on its way now, the Hospital Ship was swaying slightly and my thoughts were politely interrupted when someone said, "Now m'lad, let me see. I expect, as you're a Scot you'll be wanting to go to hospital near your home in Bonnie Scotland?"

What could I say other than suggest Glasgow!

"And if we can't get you in there, where would you like as an alternative?" he asked.

The thought of not being near home was disheartening but the next best thing was to suggest London in order to be near my rich uncle.

The orderlies were most sympathetic and the attention I got on board the Ship was outstanding.

CHAPTER 14 – [1917]

Home to Blighty

6th January – The hospital ship lay at anchor in the Solent and we were given no indication as to what time we could expect to be put ashore.

Heaving myself up a little by using a pulley installed above me, I could actually see Blighty through a porthole. The sight of just that tiny bit was sufficient to give me a thrill.

Engines now throbbed, a siren sounded but there was no immediate movement. One more siren and we were on our way. We docked at Southampton at 9am. My eyes were never so wide open as they were today as, now on the upper deck, I had time to peer at both sides of the river and convince myself that at last I was back in Blighty!

Once alongside, getting us ashore seemed no problem and we were hastily and carefully transferred to a waiting ambulance train. This left Southampton at 11.40am.

In the darkness of this wintry afternoon I could not pick out the names of the stations we were passing through.

When the train did come to a lengthy stop, was I in London or Glasgow? Neither – I was in York – roughly equidistant from both of my chosen destinations, and it was now after 10pm.

I was admitted to Fulford Military Hospital where I received a heart-warming welcome from the night staff, but the ward itself was most uninviting. No time was lost in taking me to the theatre and when I recovered my *compos mentis* I could scarcely control my emotions when I was told that it had been discovered that an operation would not be necessary – just treatment!

8th January – It being Sunday, a service was held in the ward – only the second religious service I had attended since leaving Inverness in 1914. It was wonderful to be visited by strangers and we 'boys in blue' who were able to shuffle outside and get into a car were frequently invited out to tea. These outings were most welcome – especially for those of us who had a normal appetite.

I gathered from others that this hospital was governed strictly in accordance with King's Regulations. Not that the orderlies were inattentive, but there was the impression that we would soon be required to make way for others. So much so that I pleaded to be 'marked out' – despite the necessity of having to rely on crutches. Accordingly, on the 18th January I left York for the tiny village of Bedale further north and near Northallerton. There I was welcomed into a convalescent home – a large house in the centre of the village which was given to the Red Cross by a Mr Gray, a Shipbuilder of Hartlepool. Everything possible was done for the Boys in Blue and the twenty of us agreed that it was almost like being at home. We were promised a good time – and we were not disappointed.

20th January – Whist Drive.

22nd January – Church

23rd January – Concert.

The four charming daughters of Mr Gray entertained us with song, piano, cello and violin at their enormous country house "Thorpe Perrow" hidden away amongst the trees at the end of a long drive through beautiful lawns.

24th January – Tea at Mrs Buttermacks

25th January – Red Cross Concert/Ball raised £40.

26th January – Motor run to Mrs Whitton's

27th January – Tea Party at Miss Whitton's (6 cups)

30th January – Tea at Lieut. Robson's

1st February – Concert in aid of Working Party

8th February – Haircut 3d only for the Boys

21st February – Met my brother Jack at Ripon Camp

22nd February – Harrogate with Mrs Grant

28th February – Harrogate with Pearl Gray

8th March – Accompanied village doctor on rounds
14th March – Motor outing to Leyland / Middleham
20th March – Harrogate, Sister Owen, Misses Gray
23rd March – Concert by soldiers from Catterick
25th March – Hunt Meeting at Patrick Brompton.

After three months I was able to manage without crutches but still had to rely on a stick.

Matron wanted to know why the boys didn't eat their porridge? I ventured to suggest that I knew the answer and this resulted in my accepting the responsibility of making it, although this necessitated my getting up earlier than the others, but I had the Cook for good company (a nice lady). By virtue of Matron considering me a great help, I was taken on as a most useful 'back-room boy' and became adept at peeling spuds, washing-up etc. A 'promotion' was engineered in that I became assistant to a Miss Pearl Gray. As a recompense for my hard work I was allowed certain privileges by the Doctor and Matron and mostly these resulted in my being taken for a ride – that is to say a sleigh ride! The Gray family had two tiny Shetland ponies "Dot" and "Carrie". At one time they had been used to pull Cinderella on a stage. I was driven to a nearby country lane where, to my surprise, I discovered that the two ponies and Miss Pearl Gray were waiting for me. Our sleigh-rides through the snow-covered countryside will not be forgotten – neither will the toboggan runs!

As it was rumoured that some of us would shortly be discharged, so it was arranged for us to have a photograph taken. For this purpose we Blue Boys adorned the monument in the centre of the village.

30th March – Regretfully I bid my adieus to many hospital people in Bedale as I was destined to report to Fulford Military Hospital. After a brief conversation with the doctor there I unhesitatingly suggested that I was quite fit to travel. (I wanted to go home). Consequently I left on the 12.40 from York.

31st March – Due to the two hour's wait at Newcastle and one hour's delay at Edinburgh I did not arrive in Glasgow until 10pm – too late to get home and stayed overnight at my uncle's Popular Hotel.

1st April – I reached home at 2pm but not so full of vim and vigour as I had been on my previous leave last November when I had celebrated by 21st birthday.

Making up for lost time, I was treated to the Alhambra Cinema (1st House) and the Coliseum Cinema (2nd House).

5th April – I was entertained at a farm. Nothing like variety, Pavilion this time. Cramming in as much as possible on this short leave.

9th April – On the move again with cheerios from the Minister and the Headmaster with a request to bring back more German souvenirs! I was horse-driven down to Clarkston Station and with ample time in Glasgow to re-visit my old office, but my pals had all enlisted and had been replaced by young ladies.

I left Buchanan Street Station at 10pm with several 'kilties' for company.

CHAPTER 15 – [1917]

Invergordon

19th April 1917 – There was plenty of room for all of us to stretch out but the train journey was a very cold trip North.

When I arrived at Inverness I enjoyed a much needed breakfast at Murray's Hotel. My first duty was to visit Mr Davison – my butcher friend who gave me a food parcel in November 1914 and continued to send them to me when I was in France.

After this happy reunion I left Inverness at 5.15pm and arrived at Invergordon at 8pm where I received a rather chilly reception on alighting at the Camp Station – it was snow-covered. But I got a warm welcome at the Guard Room.

The Camp had become the base of the 3rd (Reserve) Battalion of the Cameron Highlanders. It was neatly planned and the interior of the huts looked comfortable. One consolation was that it was quite near the town – not isolated as were the camps on Salisbury Plain.

Almost immediately I felt the warmth of companionship for I came into contact with a few of my 1914 pals who I had given up for 'lost' when over in France. They, like myself, were here to be 'serviced' and made available where possible to go overseas again whilst those not yet fit were employed on camp fatigues combined with light training.

13th April – I was inoculated at 2pm and to my surprise had a medical examination later in the day. The condition of my leg was such that I was classified "A3" – which meant that I was not fighting fit.

19th April – Pronounced fit for light training only.

22nd April – Church Service in town.

23rd April – Orderly Man – in other words, I was to spend the day skivvying – which entailed scrubbing tables, forms, floors etc. prior to inspection by the Orderly Officer accompanied by an NCO and the NCO in charge of the hut. No black marks. To rub it in, the Orderly Man was expected to join his hut mates in singing:

> *Wait till we go home on furlough*
> *Wait till we go home on pass*
> *We will scrub the chairs and tables*
> *Yes we will* ****************

but being a "Cameron and a Gentleman" I left unsung the final words!

After having methodically and meticulously executed the scheduled household duties I had time to sew on buttons and darn some socks – my own – I could not be bribed to do this for others.

In the evening I was free and joined up to have a game of football which did not last long for my injured leg 'went'. In a way this was a blessing in disguise for it ruled out any immediate inclusion in a draft for overseas.

24th April – Taken to Medical Hut where detailed.

29th April – Removed to Hospital in town. During the stay there we 'poor things' were visited daily by well-wishing ladies whose little gifts and company were greatly appreciated, for this makeshift 'hospital' was lacking in the expected comforts. It would have been almost impossible to accept the many invitations out to tea when we got better.

It was great news when told the Americans had declared war on Germany and this apparently created an entirely different atmosphere up at the Camp.

10th May – Homesickness and ennui prompted me once more to declare that I was feeling fine and would like to be marked out! And this was done – presumably to make way for others.

21st May – In the Cromarty Firth right in front of Alness – dream of a village with charming cottages – lay HM

Cruiser *Natal*. This, I am told, was blown up and turned turtle at Christmas 1916. It was clearly visible from the shore road and the ferryboat I took to visit the Seaforths' Depot passed quite close to it. The wreck lights fore and aft were a grim reminder of the tragedy which occurred when a large number of military and civilian guests were being entertained.

25th May – Given four hours notice to prepare to go on furlough prior to joining Draft for overseas. Left camp at 6.30pm.

26th May – With the evening departure I was able to admire the beautiful Highland scenery which was greatly enhanced by a glorious sunset. Very little sleep as it was a 'must' to see the early sunrise on a summer's day. But fourteen hours to get home! In order not to cause any undue anxiety there I did not mention that I was about to go overseas again.

31st May – Left Buchanan Street Station at 10pm and arrived once more at Invergordon – twelve hours late – when I had difficulty in convincing the Orderly Sergeant that the train delays at Dalwinnie and Aviemore were responsible for my 'overstaying my leave'.

3rd June – Whilst waiting departure date for overseas I saw on the noticeboard that a shorthand typist was required. Without hesitation I applied and was right away ushered in to see the Adjutant who in turn took me to the Colonel – the Mackintosh of Mackintosh.

He made me feel quite at ease and after a conversation with the Adjutant it was arranged for me to have a new outfit, including a kilt.

The same evening I reported to his private quarters and was again told to relax. He offered me a drink (which I refused, but I did accept a cigarette) before questioning my abilities and emphasising the importance of loyalty.

This interview resulted in my being appointed an Orderly Room Clerk, although I could get no immediate promotion as the Orderly Room Staff was already up to Establishment. In addition, I was asked if I would be prepared to deal with his private correspondence even after normal duty hours. How could I refuse?

I was more than happy with this situation, as it was no longer necessary for me to report for the usual 'square-bashing'. More important, my name was to be forthwith deleted from the 'available for overseas' list.

With such glorious summer weather, the long evenings enabled the off-duty men to indulge in all sorts of activities. Most of them sought their relaxation outside the camp, particularly down by the shore. An outstanding rendezvous was a hairdressers shop down town – for who wouldn't enjoy having their hair cut by one of the two young lady barbers?

Quite a number were getting themselves into shape for the forthcoming Regimental Games.

23rd June – The Games took place and amongst the competitors were members of the Fleet. It was pleasing to see Camerons sit with the Mackintosh to be photographed after their successes.

15th July – For the past five weeks everything went well for me and seemed likely to continue so, until I was shown the following letter:

From: *War Office London*

To: *Officer Commanding,*
          3rd Battalion Cameron Highlanders, Ivergordon

For SD 599 (SD3b) Infantry   *13 July 1917*

Sir,
*I am directed to inform you that **Private Robert Burns** of the unit under your command has been accepted for admission to an Officer Cadet Unit with a view to his subsequent appointment to a temporary commission in the Regular Army or a commission in the Territorial Force. He should, therefore, NOT be included in a draft for overseas but must be held available for early posting to an Officer Cadet Unit.*
Further instructions with regard to his Admission will be forwarded to you in due course.

    I am, Sir
    Your obedient Servant
    W D Bird, Brigadier General
    Director of Staff Duties

This War Office letter did not surprise me, as I was well aware that, many months previously, I had been recommended for a Commission. However, bearing in mind my experience of the trenches, I now found myself in a quandary. Should I go ahead with this opportunity for promotion or should I remain in Blighty in a cushy job for the rest of the war? I left my destiny in the hands of The Mackintosh and, in accordance with his judgement and guidance, he dictated the following letter:

AS/WMS   *No.16112*
To: The Secretary
WAR OFFICE, London S.W

Invergordon
16th July 1917

Sir,

With reference to Form SD599(SD3b) dated 13th July 1917 in respect of No. 14141 Pte Robert Burns return herewith, I have the honour to inform you that the candidate is at present no longer desirous of obtaining a temporary commission in the Regular or a commission in the Territorial Force, as already advised you in my <u>letter No. 15216</u>** dated the 10th July 1917, and request his name be deleted from the list of candidates awaiting admission to an Officer Cadet Unit.

I have the honour Sir
Your obedient Servant
Colonel Commanding
3rd Battalion Cameron Highlanders

**This was in reply to an instruction to present myself at the Corpus Christi College, Cambridge, which letter apparently had not been received before the War Office wrote on the 13th July 1917.

November – Since clearing up the matter of a Commission, in July, I was more than pleased with my assignment at the Camp as I had no anxieties regarding my immediate future. However, my anticipation of remaining in Scotland until the end of the war was ill-founded for I was informed, confidentially, that I would no longer be required in my present capacity.

In serious mood The Mackintosh added: "The Battalion has been ordered to go to Ireland and I shall not be going with it". I was thanked for my work in the Orderly Room and for the private and confidential work which I did for him outside normal hours.

In these seven months I saw so many of my brothers-in-arms go overseas for the first time and several come back knowing that they would never again be fit enough to go overseas. Seeing the latter brought back memories of what I and some of the others in the Camp had gone through, and although not one to 'swing the lead', I considered myself a lucky man to be in Blighty.

CHAPTER 16 – [1917/1918]

Ireland

In November we were sent to Ireland. The crossing was not one I shall easily forget. I was one of the unfortunate ones below decks. There were no seats of any description so we had to squat wherever we could find a spot large enough to accommodate both ourselves and our equipment.

Midway between Holyhead and Dublin the fun started, for as the ship swayed and dipped we were literally tossed from one side to the other and it was only those who managed to grip the centre poles who were able to avoid getting splinters. Add to this the misery of being soaked by sea water (and certain other liquids that a few men had 'brought up' involuntarily) and you'll have little difficulty realising why this was a voyage to remember, or perhaps to forget!

Our destination was Birr, a small town in the heart of the country, roughly half way between Dublin and Limerick. In an isolated position with an enormous parade ground the barracks were very old and out of date.

One bright feature of our separation from civilian life was the presence of members of the Queen Mary Army Auxiliary Corps who were mostly employed in the cookhouses, messes and in a lesser degree on typing duties. They seemed to be restrained and under severe 'curfew' but I did not think that was wholly due to the military authorities. From my own intimate knowledge, 'religion' was one factor, but the main reason I gathered was that the locals were not very happy with our 'occupation' nor by the part being played by their own girls in such uniforms.

January 1918 – Early in the new year we had a new Commanding Officer – Lieutenant Colonel Donald Walter Cameron of Lochiel. One morning I was told to report to the Adjutant – Captain McCrae who in a friendly manner outlined what was in store for me and I accompanied him into the CO's room. 'Lochiel' as he was generally referred to, had apparently been advised of my close contact with The Mackintosh and he forthwith gave me the opportunity of continuing in a similar capacity.

I informed him that in order to meet the wishes of The Mackintosh I agreed to withdraw my application for a commission but having left Scotland I felt I ought to re-apply. However, as a result of our *tête-à-tête* I left myself in Lochiel's hands and considered it would have been imprudent not to acquiesce to his suggestion that I remain with him.

In a military sense nothing unusual took place at these barracks but outside one had the feeling that we had to be on the *qui vive.*

One topic of conversation by rank and file was the almost continual presence of a Great Dane which accompanied the Major almost everywhere whether in or out of the barracks. This animal was a menace, for when the men were on parade whether at 'attention' or 'at ease' it made a habit of licking bare knees or sniffing in the wrong quarters! Perhaps it was it merely trying to satisfy its curiosity!

When anyone mentions Guinness, my thoughts not only go back to the sight of barges on the Liffey, laden with it, but also to Birr Barracks.

It was quite common to return to a barrack room on a cold night and find someone holding a poker in the open fire until it became red-hot before dipping it into a glass of stout to make a frothy night-cap. For all his coaxing, the QMS could never induce me to 'have a wee sip'.

March – We packed up and went to Ballyvonare Camp near Buttevant in County Cork. We were quite near the village of Doneraile. The comparatively new huts were all that could be desired and were located in an unrestricted area allowing plenty of freedom without having to apply for a 'pass out'.

Being exempt from the usual military duties I had ample time to stroll over the undulating countryside where there was very little sign of habitation.

Occasionally (two of us) would come across a crofter's cottage where could be seen an old man or woman, sitting contentedly on the front-of-the-house stone step puffing away at a cheek-warmer in the shape of a white clay pipe with a broken shank. Geese and chickens wandered about unhindered to the accompaniment of the snorting of an unseen pig. It seemed such a peaceful sight.

Suddenly we found ourselves under attack by a gaggle of geese – there must have been between fifty and a hundred of them – swirling round and round making concerted dives to within inches of our heads, compelling us to take evasive action by diving under a roadside hedge. There we remained until the winged attackers changed their tactics and decided to take on another group of innocents. The cacophony had been ear-splitting throughout the unprovoked onslaught – almost as bad as the noise of bursting shells in France – and not at all what we had expected in a quiet Irish village. On making enquiries at a nearby cottage as to why we had been pursued, we were merely informed that there were no nesting places in the vicinity.

April – We were still enjoying a rather peaceful life but became anxious when news leaked through that our 7th Battalion (now in the Arras area) had been bearing the brunt of a heavy attack. It was later revealed that they had been pushed back and this caused uneasiness – particularly amongst those of us who had been overseas – wondering how our 1914 mates were faring.

23rd April – We were told to get ready to move. Where were we going now? In a very few hours we found ourselves in Limerick, where we had been called in to replace a regiment which, we were told by some of the inhabitants, had to 'get out quick'.

We were accommodated at Strand Barracks which had a 2-star rating compared to those we had vacated in 'The Bog' at Birr. We had an unexpectedly friendly reception – no doubt due to our Pipe Band enlivening our arrival plus the fact that we were Highlanders. Suffice it to say that, so we were informed during our fraternising interludes, there was no longer a disturbed atmosphere in this big city.

It was very disconcerting to hear stories of soldiers having been thrown from the bridge into the River Shannon and how others, to protect themselves, had carried an entrenching-tool handle up their sleeves (these could not be seen by the Guard when going out after duty).

Being in the West of Ireland was like a holiday compared to the tension we had experienced in other parts. What could be more pleasant than a leisurely stroll along the banks of the River Shannon – most particularly at sunset – watching a lone fisherman in his coracle dragging in his net with (or without) a much sought after salmon?

The very mention of Ireland brings back memories of those views up and down that wide majestic river. If a walk through this lovely town was preferred, there one could buy pork sausages, delicious cream caramels and Cleeve's condensed milk – the very same stuff that had sustained me whilst in training on Salisbury Plain or when clamouring for something to eat when in the trenches.

10th June – This pleasant seven week interlude came to an end and we returned to our Ballyvonare huts where we settled in without a repetition of the muddy drawbacks on our arrival there in March. Those who had remained behind to tidy up were undoubtedly happy that we had come back to break the monotony and we were grateful for the smashing meal that awaited us.

Always with an innate desire to 'see the world and get paid for it' a possible visit to the Lakes of Killarney as an outstanding feature was contemplated. Accordingly we (three of us) took the train at Mallow but broke our journey, getting off at Rathbone Station.

As we appeared to be undecided as to our intentions we were more or less coerced into accepting the offer of a jaunting-car, the driver suggested that he take us to a well-known beauty spot. The cost of the hire seemed reasonable and we accepted the offer.

We were having an interesting drive through the lovely countryside until five or six individuals, with guns, coming from both sides of a quiet road ordered all of us to get down and we did this only too willingly.

They did not search us, or ask us for money – but we were compelled to take off our boots! We were then told to consider ourselves lucky to be wearing kilts, inferring that had we not been Scots, something much worse would have happened to us. Having assured themselves that we were not carrying firearms we were told to scram – quick. Needless to say, we did as they asked without argument!

There was no alternative but to start hiking it, so with our tails between our legs, off we went, only too glad that we had not been subjected to any rough treatment. Fortunately, we had not gone far before we got a lift back to Mallow where two MPs, seeing us without our boots, laughingly accepted our story. Driving as near as possible up to the camp, I made my way inconspicuously to my hut and lost no time in getting something on my blistered feet. I thereupon reported the matter to the Adjutant and typed a statement which was passed on to Lochiel. There was no delay in the issue of new boots, but that was the nearest I ever got to the Lakes of Killarney!

Undaunted by our previous experience, at a later date, two of us decided to set off on an anywhere-you-like late evening circular tour. As it was already getting dark, we made our way to a railway station. However, we were too late – we had missed the last train and it would have been unwise to attempt walking back. The railway porter could only after one solution, and that was to, "Stay here 'til four o'clock in the morning when a light engine will be passing through. I'll try to stop it..." We waited, and sure enough, in the small hours of the morning, it came and it stopped.

The driver, who had relations in Scotland, was a bit hesitant in allowing us to get on, but eventually agreed to help us, provided we sat among the coals and hid ourselves when instructed, on approaching certain places. As he neared his destination, we were obliged to alight close to a narrow road. We were lucky in that it had not been necessary to conceal ourselves in the coal but one can imagine the state of our knees etc. We were able to smarten ourselves up a bit, and due to the fact that I was an Orderly Room-wallah, there was no hold-up at the Guard Room.

July – We were now blessed with real summer weather and after the normal duties and exercises many men could be seen training for the forthcoming Sports Day. Even some of those who had considered themselves 'finished for good' were endeavouring to get fit so as to participate in something.

On the day of the Sports Meeting, Lochiel introduced me to Lady Hermione (his wife) who presented the prizes. Thereafter there were many occasions when I had the privilege of having conversations with her – mostly about our respective families.

There could be no doubt that the incidents at the Easter Rising of 1916 were still haunting some Irish people, although the most part of the locals were very friendly. Nevertheless, we had to be on the alert at all times, which was emphasised when I and some others visited the City of Cork.

It was decided that the best diversion would be a visit to the cinema. It seemed to be packed but there were very few uniforms to be seen. The film broke down at least four times but the 'entertainment' continued. We were sitting in the front row of the stalls, the screen being about twenty feet away. Two tiny dogs were sitting on the floor directly in front of us seemingly enjoying the film but no sooner had the film 'gone off' and the hall thrown into darkness than a duet was given by the dogs. All this to the accompaniment of a derisive male audience. Once was bad enough but at each of the film breaks louder and louder were the canine interludes. Although 'God Save The King' was screened at the end of the performance, very briefly and without any musical accompaniment it would have been asking for trouble had we not behaved like the other members of the audience and remained seated. It was still light when we left this cinema but we did not venture to see the sights of the City, preferring to return unmolested to the barracks.

August – It was disappointing news for we old members of the "Shiny Seventh" when we learnt that it had been absorbed into the 6th Battalion.

Another surprise was the arrival of the WAACs, although unfortunately there were not enough to go round. As at Birr the ladies proved most useful from the domestic angle. I was one of the lucky ones, for I was allocated a female assistant in the Orderly Room. Although she was not quite five feet tall she went over 'big' – her name was McGillicuddy.

September – A dance was held in the village hall – something we were waiting for and it was well patronised. The young lady pianist appeared to be in difficulties when turning over her music and I did not need to be asked twice to get up on the platform to help her. When the dance was over I was actually invited to take her home. As this did not involve going out of my way I willingly consented, although it was dark.

She told me her father was 'in the Police' so I thought I would have no trouble and in fact when we reached the door of her home I could see over it distinctly the monogram 'RUC'.

Being almost 'time-up', I had to hurry back to Camp. I had gone only a few yards when I was pounced upon by a gang of youths. Fortunately, luck was with me, for my pals were following close behind, and in double-quick time they set about my would-be assailants, more than getting their own back!

Apart from this slight disturbance, the geese attack, the jaunting-car 'hold-up' and the 'interference' in Cork City there was less excitement than we expected in view of the dire warnings we had been given, to be constantly on the lookout for whatever might be 'round the corner'.

CHAPTER 17 – [1918/1919]

Armistice

November – Since coming to Ireland a year previously we had been subjected to rigorous military discipline, but the noticeable relaxation of this lately had been responsible for the circulation of hopeful rumours that the war would soon be over.

Towards the end of October I was confined to the Camp Hospital with a fever. Conversation there was mostly about peace. When would it come? It was decided to set up a sweepstake and the one who had the date nearest to the Armistice would be the winner. I chose my birthday, the 12th November, but as this was considered too far away I became the target for much derisive laughter, along with pillows, boots etc, although, of course, I had the last laugh when the armistice was eventually signed on November 11th.

With the marked changes in our day-to-day activities it was no surprise to us when it was officially confirmed that 'it was all over' and nothing could suppress the enthusiasm that pervaded the camp – particularly from those who had been liable to go overseas again.

Uppermost in everybody's mind now, was the prospect of returning home to their normal lives and their peacetime occupations, especially the married men (understandably) who were dying to get home to their families. As the days passed there were many discontented grumblings at the delay in being given any clue as to the actual date of our demobilisation. Of course, in my position, I was privy to this top-secret information, but it would have been a gross breach of confidence to even hint at what I knew.

To counteract the increasing anxiety, many diversions were sought, such as sports, football, a dance and a concert. The Pipers always put up a good show and enhanced the events which certainly helped to lift the morale of the men.

Lessons were also given to those wishing to learn or improve their Highland Dancing technique. It was an eye-opener (from more than one point of view!) to witness the swirling o' the kilts to the skirling o' the pipes. Who could fail to celebrate St Andrews Day? Educational classes were arranged and for my part I was more than pleased when given an opportunity to give French lessons to about thirty 'students'.

This innovation was welcomed by me but, unfortunately, it came to an end all too soon as it clashed with my Orderly Room and other important duties.

Gradually the establishment diminished and Lochiel informed me that he was about to relinquish command and return to Achnacarry. I was greatly saddened to hear this. I had taken great pleasure in serving him and had also enjoyed the friendly chats I had with Lady Hermione, who appeared interested in my welfare.

Lochiel discussed with me the possibility of finding a 'niche' whereby he could make use of my adaptability on his Achnacarry Estate in the event of my having any difficulty gaining immediate re-employment after being demobbed. Whilst appreciating his offer, I could not accept it, as I had already committed myself to resuming my former position. In addition, my sole desire was to get home to be with my family – in preference to living what would surely be a life of semi-isolation in the Highlands. I found the 'private and confidential' work most interesting and this, along with my other duties dealing with matters of a military nature widened my knowledge considerably. One important factor too was that because I had been thus employed, my secretarial skills had not deteriorated – but increased.

With no anxieties now regarding the possibility of having to go overseas and the prospect of an early return to Civvy Street, we could look forward to Christmas and New Year celebrations with renewed hope, and hopefully at home with our families. As it turned out, however, I had to be content with an Irish Christmas.

6th January – The Regimental Colours which had been brought from the Depot at Inverness were unfurled and ceremoniously re-presented to the Battalion.

14th February – Lochiel's command officially terminated today when Lt. Col Brown took over. The pending changes and the transfer of personnel entailed increased Orderly Room work – which I much preferred to the kill-the-time parades and the tidying up of the Camp.

The WAACs had done a good job in the various cookhouses and messes and it was easy to see that their presence had been welcomed by all ranks. We could not let them go without showing some appreciation and this was done by arranging a dance. As a souvenir each of the girls was presented with a much sought after Cameron badge.

The Mackintosh of Mackintosh had been in command of the 3rd Battalion for over three years before handing over to Lochiel who remained in charge until February 1919.

It was the responsibility of this Reserve Battalion not only to receive, equip and train raw recruits but also, with patience, get back to normal condition those men who had been hospitalised or otherwise affected by service overseas.

Indeed, over 15,000 men had been sent over to either strengthen battalions or replace the constantly recurring casualties.

With regard to the 7th Battalion – we left Inverness in 1914 just over 1,100 strong. During the course of the war, including replacements, 1,100 men lost their lives. How many of the original battalion members had survived the war was impossible to tell.

It was whilst attached to the 44th Brigade Headquarters in France and later, involved in the Orderly Rooms in Scotland and Ireland that I became cognisant of certain facts which I had to regard a secret.

Obviously overseas it would have been indiscreet to have kept the minutely shorthand notes in my possession. Nevertheless, once back in the UK, I continued making notes and when I reached home on leave I enveloped these for future reference. Hence it is that I am furnished with data which gives me mixed feelings whenever I am asked, "What did you do in the war Daddy?"

c/6445

Army Form Z. 21.

CERTIFICATE of* { Discharge
Transfer to Reserve
Disembodiment
Demobilization } on Demobilization.

Regtl. No. S/14141 .... Rank ... Cpl

Names in full ..... Burns Robert
(Surname first)

Unit and Regiment or Corps
from which
*Discharged
Transferred to Reserve } 3 Cameron Highrs

Enlisted on the ..... 6th November ... 1914

For ..... Cameron Highrs
(Here state Regiment or Corps to which first appointed)

Also served in .....

Only Regiments or Corps in which the Soldier served since August 6th, 1914, are to be stated.
If inapplicable, this space is to be ruled through in ink and initialled.

Nil

†Medals and
Decorations
awarded during
present engage-
ment } .....

*Has
Has not } served Overseas on Active Service.

Place of Rejoining in
case of emergency } ..... Kinross ..... Medical Category ... Bii

Specialist Military
qualifications } ..... Year of birth .. 1895

He is* { Discharged
Transferred to Army Reserve
Disembodied
Demobilized } on 1st May ... 1919

in consequence of Demobilization.

..... Morrison Lieut .....Signature and Rank.

Officer i/c .. Infantry .. Records. .. No. 1 Dist Perth ..(Place).

* Strike out whichever is inapplicable.   † The word "Nil" to be inserted when necessary.

(20996).   Wt. W 8211—P.P. 2329.   3,000m.   1/19.   D & S.   (E 1256.)

CHAPTER 18 – [1919]

Demobbed

6th March 1919 – The outstanding feature of our fourteen months in Ireland was watching the Pipers leading the battalion out of Ballyvonare Camp on its way to Edinburgh.

I was one of the unlucky ones having to remain behind, but nevertheless it was uplifting to see my pals in such high spirits thrilled with the knowledge that they were at long last on their way 'out'.

With the WAACs gone too and only a few Regulars left behind with myself, the Camp resembled a ghost-town.

We were given to understand that those with jobs to go to would be the first to be released but despite my having been 'listed' months ago I was still there!

Nevertheless, I looked back upon my year's sojourn in Ireland as being more of an extended leave when I considered what had in the meantime been taking place across the Channel.

Whilst impatiently awaiting for some good news, I received a letter and testimonial from Lochiel. Three more weeks elapsed before I finally got away from Ballyvonare.

From County Cork to Auld Reekie is a long way, but although unaccompanied I regarded the journey as a pleasure trip. Travel weary, I was thankful that the late hour of my arrival at the comparatively new Redford Barracks in Edinburgh necessitated my staying overnight.

The following day, 3rd April I was handed the Commanding Officer's 'farewell' which read:

14141 – Cpl R Burns, 3rd Reserve Bn. Camerons

During the last four years of War, all ranks of the British Army have travelled a long and difficult road together – many have fallen by the way, whilst others have suffered severely from wounds and sickness. The enemy have been beaten by the valour, tenacity and discipline of the British Army and our Allies after a struggle such as the world has never seen before. You are now about to be demobilised and will soon be home once again.

IN THE NAME OF THE BRITISH ARMY I take this opportunity to thank you for what you have done, to wish you farewell and the best of fortune on your return to civil life.

> *For O. C. Commanding*
> *(Unit) 3rd RES. BN Cameron Highlanders*
> *3/4/1919*

Despite wishing to get rid of the uniform and equipment without any loss of time, I just could not accept the awful 'demob suit' offered me – even though it was free – so I chose to go home in uniform.

After four and a half years in the Army (instead of the six months predicted) I was delighted when handed my 'Certificate of Demobilisation and Transfer to Army Reserve' on 1st May 1919. Being still slightly incapacitated I was classified 'Category B2'.

Now belatedly demobbed and with a Railway Warrant actually in my hand, there was no withholding my burning desire to get home.

I telephoned our home number, Eaglesham 1 (the first telephone to be installed in our village) giving my approximate time of my arrival.

My parents had no doubt been overjoyed in spreading the news of my impending arrival, for when the bus came to a halt at the end of our drive, a little crowd of children was waiting: the school had been given a half day's holiday. Alas, on this occasion I had no German helmets or any other souvenirs.

As time rolled on, it was not easy to convince myself that my Army days were now definitely over.

So long as I have to carry a 'Blighty leg', how shall I ever forget that awful war, or the marvellous comradeship of the men of the Cameron Highlanders?

My thoughts will always be of those who went out but did not return...

A sad footnote: my pal Jimmy, who enlisted with me in 1914 and survived the war unscathed, tragically died two months after returning home.

Appendices

Insignia of the Highland Regiments

Black Watch

Cameron

Gordon

Seaforth

Towns & Villages in France

The places mentioned below are those that I passed through in the course of my wartime service. At the time I visited them, some were untouched by the war; others had been slightly or severely damaged whilst many more were completely razed. There were many places where, on the way 'up' we enjoyed a hearty welcome, only to return months later to discover that, in certain instances, the villages were now non-existent. Despite their ruined condition, it was sometimes possible to use the cellars for Battalion or Brigade Headquarters and they also provided cover from the shelling for troops moving 'up'.

Ablaincourt	Brunay
Albert	Burbue
Allouagne	Busnes
Amiens	Butte de Warlecourt
Annequin	Candus
Auchel	Canteleux

Auchy au Bois

Autheux

Averdoingt

Bailleul aux Corneilles

Bapaume

Bazentin le Petit

Becourt

Behencourt

Bethune

Boulogne

Bresle

Bruay-en-Artois

Franvillers

Frechencourt

Gonnehem

Gosnay

Gouy en Ternois

Hallencourt

Hazebrouck

Heilly

Honvel

Houchin

Houlle

Hulluch

Hurionville

La Boiselle

Cauchy La Tour

Chocques

Contalmaison

Courcelette

Coyecques

Cumem

Dieval

Division

Ecquedecques

Fervin Palfart

Finevillers

Flechin

Martinpuich

Mazingarbe

Mericourt

Millencourt

Mirvaux

Monchy Breton

Naours

Noeix les Mines

Noyelles

Occoches

Ourton

Perfay Bellory

Philosophe

Pont de Briques

La Buissiere	Quality Street
La Houssoys	Rebreuve
La Trieuloye	Rely
Labourse	Rouen
Lavieville	Sailly Labourse
Le Perlecques	Septenville
Le Sarz	St Omer
Les Brebis	St Venant
Lieres	Talmas
Lillers	Thiepval
Loos	Vaudricourt
Lozinghem	Vermelles
Mametz	Verquin
Maroc	Watten Eperlecques

I would like to express my gratitude to Lieutenant Colonel A. A. Fairrie, curator of the regimental museum of the Queen's Own Highlanders, Fort George, Inverness for his help and assistance in drawing up this list of French towns. I would also like to thank the museum's trustees for granting their permission to use the painting which appears on the front cover.

A studio portrait of the author taken in London in 1926.

Life after Demob

After demob I came to London from Scotland and stayed with my parents in their recently purchased hotel in the West End. Frank St Leger, Nelly Melba's pianist, happened to be one of the hotel guests at that time, and one day as I was sitting strumming a Spanish guitar, who should walk in but Nelly herself. We had several conversations after that before she asked me if I would care to manage her protegée, Gabrielle Ray, who, I was informed, was leading dancer at the Empire Leicester Square. I acquiesced, and that was my initiation into the music halls. For many weeks, it was Empire here, Pavilion there, and so on... until Gabrielle went to America.

I was a circus and dance hall manager for Bertram Mills between 1921 in 1927. This work was seasonal, of course, and after Gabrielle went abroad I joined *The Performer* (magazine of the Variety Artistes Federation) in Charing Cross Road, where John Warr (another Scot) was editor. When I gave that up, my wife took my place and dealt with the VAF chiefly.

When I left Bertram Mills at the end of the 1923/24 season, I was asked if I would like to be ticket controller of the forthcoming British Empire Exhibition at Wembley, so I was there for the duration. After the exhibition, it was back to my insurance agency in Victoria Street. I was also able to assist in hotel management in the West End, and devoted some time to investments in foreign exchange in Lower Regent Street. I didn't find this exciting enough, however, and as a result of answering advertisements, I became acting manager of 'Fred Karno's Follies'. With the usual weekly stands, I travelled the country North, South, East and West. It was a happy life. The landladies were all called 'Mrs Whatsit' and it never cost more than 18 shillings a week. The barrow boys met you at the station and escorted you to your digs, charging sixpence for each case. They would even be there at two or three in the morning when the train arrived!

Another opportunity came when I was asked if I spoke French. I did.

"Well," said my questioner, "the Royal Automobile Club has an advert in the paper." Immaculately attired at the interview, I was told that the position was mine. After two weeks in Pall Mall, I was appointed assistant to the one and only representative in Nice on the French Riviera. The office was right opposite the pier (which is no longer there). It was a wonderful experience and I was sorry to leave, but Bertram Mills relied on me to rejoin him and take over management of the Olympia Dance Hall, Kensington.

There being no television in those days, ballrooms and dance halls were where people went for entertainment. I decided it was time to stop roving and became manager of the Astoria Ballroom, Charing Cross Road. One day there, I bumped into a Major Green and his son 'Wee Hughie' and took them in for coffee. I asked Hughie what he wanted to be when he grew up. 'A comedian', he said.

I left the Astoria in 1928 to take over the new ballroom, the casino in Liverpool — the largest dance hall in Britain — but after a year it was converted into a skating rink, so I left to return to London where I again took up cinema management. For me, this was not very exciting and I had no difficulty in being appointed manager of Cricklewood Dance Hall and Skating Rink.

In days gone by I had played the Regent Bradford, and following its takeover by ABC, I went back again as manager. What a beautiful building compared with the one I had managed in Beverley Road, Hull a few years previously. From there, I went to the Savoy, Darley Street and records show that I managed at least 15 cinemas.

Sometimes there were 'personal appearances', when it was my pleasure to present the stars of the films to the audience. Apart from British actors, there were a few from

America too. On one occasion at Salisbury, Bob Hope said to me "I guess you are Bob, too." I replied, "Wrong! I am Bob ONE!" Was there applause?

It was a wonderful life until my retirement in 1955. It had really been an education meeting people from all over England and seeing the country. That was my life in the entertainment business... but there was much more to come in the next 40 years! Just as an example, in 1967 I found myself in Paris on the stage of the Follies Bergeres. Dressed in a kilt with a background of 40 nudes, I was doing the 'Highland Fling'. My foot caught on my skirt and I went sprawling. Yvette, the star, picked me up. Worth the money?

Now I have no worries and am thoroughly enjoying my retirement in the luxurious residential home of the Cinematograph and Television Fund, Glebelands House, Wokingham, Berkshire.

Robert Burns, 1996

Burns' Model Lodging Houses

When 102 year-old Robert Burns stood up to acknowledge the applause of the audience at a charity concert in Glasgow's Royal Concert Hall recently, little did they know that his family had housed hundreds of their ancestors for less than five pence a night.

Very proudly, Robbie will tell how his grandfather established Burns' Model Lodging Houses in Glasgow.

"Each man had his own cubicle, a place for the man in a space for his things," said Robbie. A string of four lodging houses was set up, offering accommodation at a modest price which was affordable to the ordinary working man.

"Every night between 600 and 800 men slept in the model lodging houses, but the only one I remember seeing was in James Watt Street as a boy."

There is nothing today which equates to the standards and scale of the model lodging houses and hotels set up by people like Robbie's grandfather.

"I never remember seeing my grandfather. I was born in November 1895. From what my parents told me, he was well-known in Glasgow. My uncles carried on the lodging house business and extended it," said Robbie.

One famous family establishment was the Exhibition Hotel in Clyde Street, Anderston Cross.

"When I was a boy, they charged seven pence, nine pence and one shilling a night, explained Robbie, referring to pre-decimal pounds, shillings and pence. Today's equivalent of one shilling is 5p. Owned by his uncle, Tom Broughton, a brother of his mother, the hotel had been named after one in Cork.

"I remember when I worked in an insurance office in Buchanan Street I'd rush down to my uncle's hotel for lunch. It was cheap at sixpence, but I got it for half price, being family," said the World War I veteran. "I'd have a good plate of soup and steak and kidney pie and rice pudding for today's equivalent of 1p."

In July 1847, William Burns, secretary of the Glasgow Association for Establishing Lodging Houses for the working classes, faithfully recorded the details of costs and charges in the Mitchell Street houses which they had hurriedly leased for three years.

"The house is on four floors and can accommodate 600 individuals. A lodger can procure a comfortable and clean bed for three pence and a wholesome and plain breakfast or supper for two pence. He can sleep securely in a haven, a place perfectly private and free from witnessing scenes of intoxication and immorality," writes Mr Burns. The lodger would also have "the privilege of reading several of the most useful and instructive publications of the day and shortly will have a more extended selection of books," he reports. He also states that, "no ardent spirits are admitted."

Within days, the Association knew the place was too small. They then bought ground between St Andrew's Square and Glasgow Green for a purpose-built Model Lodging House to accommodate '400 - 500 lodgers in comfort combined with cheapness.'

Their aim was to accommodate the estimated 5,000 people living in grossly overcrowded and unhygienic conditions in 'the Wynds and Streets upon the South Side of the Trongate in High Street, Gallowgate and Canon. These places consist of lodging houses which constitute the very worst parts. They are crowded with inmates, men and women, promiscuously huddled together. There is a total absence of everything like the ventilation or cleanliness necessary to contribute to common decencies of life.'

There was also the matter of 'fever raging with fearful severity,' because people lived in these conditions without change of bedclothes - 'if that is what such rags as are provided may be called.' The question of what to do about these 'serious evils' was answered by 'administering to the welfare of the working classes' by forming the Association to provide better lodgings. 'Accommodating 5,000 is no easy task,' admitted the Association. But they went about it with a will.

They set up and maintained lodging houses in various parts of the city, 'providing comfortable, cheap accommodation for the working classes, including strangers to the city in search of employment or in transit to other places.' Public subscriptions and donations from 'upward of £5' were called for. George and James Burns contributed £10. Donations of £100 were received from: Wm Baird & Co, Charles Tennant & Co, Wm Dixon and John Dennistoun among others.

In 1875, twenty years before Robert Burns was born, the Lord Provost of Glasgow, the Hon James Bain, chaired the annual general meeting of the Glasgow Model Lodging Houses Association. The report recorded that, a total of 182,326 people had stayed in their lodging houses in Greendyke Street, Macalpine Street and Carrick Street. 'An average of 500 persons a night,' notes the report. One man had stayed in the Greendyke Street Lodging House for 25 years and one woman had lived in the Camck Street house for 15, years. 'These Model Lodging Houses are not for wayfarers and strangers only, but are the only home of many poor men and women.'

The Association was very profitable. Income for the year to March 1874 was over £2,526. Expenditure was over £1,911 and the excess was invested in U.S. Bonds and Pennsylvania Railway Bonds.

The illustrious citizens who made up the Association also recommended that 'looking at present want of cheap accommodation in the city and the benefits conferred by the Model Lodging Houses, we earnestly recommend to the public the erection of lodging houses similar to those belonging to the Association.'

In the next century - around the early 1930s - Robbie's uncle, Tom Gordon was still in the business of providing good accommodation.

"He built the Adelphi Hotel at the corner of Renfield Street and Argyle Street on the opposite side from Central Station," recollected Robert.

"I once came up from London for a holiday there. My uncle also had the Popular Hotel – off Hope Street, and another one in the Trongate where I often had lunch and paid the same price as everyone else. Occasionally I'd stay there when I went to evening classes at Hendry's College to learn shorthand and typing," he added.

Robert's uncle went to London with £100 and built the Shaftsbury Avenue Hotel and later the Mount Royal Hotel in Marble Arch. Robbie followed him to London.

Robbie is amazingly fit for his age. Today he lives happily in a luxurious retirement home for cinema and television personnel in Berkshire. Always the gentleman, he still knows how to charm the ladies. After the charity concert in Glasgow, at least half a dozen women approached him to chat.

"I'd love to get to know you if I were 40 years younger," he said to each as he doffed his hat, respectfully.

He followed in the family footsteps and in, his working life has managed hotels, theatres, cinemas, roller skating rinks, dance halls and billiard halls. When he retired at the age of 59 he bought a hotel. When his wife died in 1963 he took himself off to Paris where he worked – voluntarily – for eleven years with the poor and elderly who were cared for by a charity called *Les Petits Freres des Pauvres* (The Little Brothers of the Poor).

"I loved that," he says honestly. "I felt happy then. I would have to climb four flights of stairs to attend to some old folk and did practically everything for their comfort. But it didn't matter. I was helping someone. I was learning French and seeing the world."

He later went to Morocco with the same charity and was also sent to French-speaking Canada twice and Chicago four times to help organise their community ventures.

Robbie was in Glasgow as guest of honour at Eaglesham Gala Day. His parents had set up the Gordon Boarding Establishment in the village in 1907 and had run a popular dance hall.

"I remember they knocked down the walls of several cottages to make a big space and on Saturday night the milkmaids arrived with their short skirts and black stockings and the farm lads with their polished boots. The orchestra was my sister at the piano plus someone at the melodeon or the concertina. I went round them with my cap and got sixpence off everyone."

When he started work as a clerk in Glasgow he had to walk four miles to the railway station at Clarkston.

"That took an hour," he said. The exercise, he reckons, has been a contributing factor to his long life and good health. "And, I've always worked," he added.

His busy working life led him to being invited to the House of Lords, the House of Commons, No 10 Downing Street and Buckingham Palace on various occasions.

*This article by Grace Franklin, first appeared in **The Big Issue** in 1998.*

*Robert in conversation with Princess Alexandra
at a Buckingham Palace garden party on the 22nd of July 1999. She is
inspecting one of his medals – France's Legion D'Honneur*

The Further Adventures of Robert Burns Esq

The following piece first appeared in the 1996 Annual Report of the Cinematograph and Television Benevolent Fund (CTBF).

Such was the interest in the article about Robert Burns in last year's Annual Report, that "in response to popular demand" it is clearly appropriate to give details of the recent activities of this most remarkable man - the Fund's oldest male beneficiary and a resident at 'Glebelands'.

The latter half of 1996 was a particularly busy time for Robert – in early July he laid a wreath at the Thiepval Memorial to commemorate the 80th Anniversary of the Battle of the Somme in which he fought, later that month he was one of only six wearing the 1914/15 medal at the Not Forgotten Association Garden Party at Buckingham Palace and during the next couple of months he was much in demand addressing school children and Old Comrades'

Reunions. He found time at the Chester Reunion to cast a knowledgeable and critical eye over the Tower of London Exhibition, which was on tour of the North West.

He was interviewed by SSVC Television in early October in connection with a programme being prepared for transmission to British Forces worldwide on Remembrance Day and later that month he went off to France again for a four day film shoot with the Dutch Television Company Network, who were making a programme about World War I. A few days later he was off on British Legion business on visits to the Lake District, Preston, Liverpool and Wigan.

In November he was interviewed by the *Sunday Express*, was military consultant to a production of *Journey's End*, attended the Wokingham Remembrance Day Service and, as reported elsewhere, was the 'star' of the 50th Royal Film Performance on the occasion of his 101st birthday. His determination to stay at the subsequent Café de Paris reception until the early hours was explained in part by the queue of young ladies who were anxious to give him a birthday kiss.

"Most enjoyable," he was heard to say.

December was a never-ending series of lunches, receptions and other festive occasions, which Robert greatly appreciated, but he was particularly impressed when he met some of the Lady Veterans of World War I at the British Legion Party.

Pinewood Studios gave their generous Christmas Party at 'Glebelands', which was especially well received by the residents and no prizes for guessing who was one of the last to leave! Christmas Eve, Christmas Day, Boxing Day all received favourable mention in his diary, but are only of passing interest to a true Scotsman, so it was the New Year's Eve Party about which he really enthused.

Burns Night at 'Glebelands' in late January was, as usual, organised by Robert, and woe betide the Sassenachs who got the procedure wrong – even now he is busy planning the 1998 event.

If the secret of long life lies in keeping busy then there is no finer example than Robert Burns Esq. In addition to the activities mentioned, he has received visits from family and friends from the USA, Australia and France and is presently planning his summer 1997 programme. Everyone associated with the CTBF is extremely proud of him; we admire his courage, the example he sets and his single-mindedness, but most of all his concern for others.

[signature]

[signature]

Somme Day Lunch
1st July 2000

Luncheon in honour of
Mr Robert Burns,
7th Battalion Cameron Highlanders,
(12th November 1895)
and his comrades who served on the Somme

A signed menu from one of the many social occasions Robert attended –
this time it was a dinner held in his honour.

A Newsletter from Glebelands

This is, primarily to tender my thanks to all those who gratefully reminded me of my happy youth and sent me their best wishes and exhorted me to "Keep right on to the end of the road".

At 12.01am on 1st January, in accordance with custom, suitably bottled, I strolled around, but no one could join me! Not downhearted, I organised a Burns Night so we had a cheerful beginning to 1999. With the memory of a peacock I'll endeavour to record just what happened up until now.

On April Fool's Day with other residents, I went to Broadmoor. Is it a prison or a hospital? The inmates staged an enjoyable play. Before we got in we were "searched" and likewise coming out.

On April 2nd, General Joffre's granddaughter phoned, congratulating me on receiving the Legion d'Honneur medal.

From June 17th to 21st we ex-veterans visited Belgium and France. We visited Napoleon's Tomb at Les Invalides in Paris and were entertained in the British Embassy. We then visited the Tomb of the Unknown Soldier and took part in the ceremony that takes place at 6.30pm every day. There I met Natalyne Joffre who thanked me for giving certain information to include in her stories of the war.

On July 1st I was selected to take part in a ceremony at the Cenotaph. All the traffic in Whitehall was stopped while the ceremony took place. Afterwards, Sir Winston Churchill presented me to the spectators as 'A hero of the Battle of the Somme'! I was introduced to about fifteen soldiers of the Commonwealth. Later I had lunch in the House of Lords. I was the only ex-soldier at this outstanding event.

On July 8th, Lady Angela phoned, asking me if I was going to Scotland, as the Queen Mother was about to go to Balmoral.

On July 15th I attended a Garden Party at Buckingham Palace (my fifth visit there) where I met the Queen Mother.

July 22nd I was at Buckingham Palace again. I spoke with Princess Alexandra this time.

On July 21st Television Francaise cameramen came to film me.

I went to Scotland on August 24th for a fortnight, mostly Glasgow and the Firth of Clyde, where I visited my birthplace in Gourock. It was a marvellous holiday. I met Vivienne, whose grandfather was in the Camerons, as I was, in the First World War – the same platoon!

On September 22nd I was invited to the Royal Hospital Chelsea for the "Big Brew Up". There I met Lords, Ladies and high-ranking officers of the Forces. This time I was photographed having a chat with Prince Michael of Kent. Meridian, the Television Company, took me to their studios in Southampton on November 7th, where I was extensively filmed for "Spotlight".

With 12 other veterans, on November 8th, I went to the Imperial War Museum. Three hours were taken up with filming and discussions. It was all seen and heard on TV the same evening.

On November 11th Natalyne Joffre phoned me from Paris, stating that she had seen me on Television Francaise in the morning, as did three other friends.

November 12th – my birthday – was celebrated graced by the pleasure of the presence of my son, 'Young Robert' and of course his wife Vera. I had a message from Her Majesty the Queen Mother and another from Sir Winston Churchill.

I took part in the Royal British Legion Church Parade on November 14th (Remembrance Sunday). We then went on to the Citadel at Reading for the Salvation Army Service. There I thanked the Salvation Army for their wonderful attention when I was almost 'out' on the Somme battlefield.

Glebelands, where Robert spent his final years.

A few days late, my birthday celebrations were held on November 16th with the Chelsea Pensioners, at the Royal Hospital Chelsea. It is a most interesting hospital, housing 387 old soldiers – the oldest being 98.

On November 17th I was on the move again to Worthing with a few veterans to have lunch with the Lord Lieutenant of Sussex and the Mayor.

November 20th saw me being taken by Rolls Royce to Reading Football Club's stadium, At half time I was 'paraded' before the spectators and on the field I drew the winning raffle ticket from an elaborate drum. The electronic board displayed the message "Welcome to Robert Burns - 104". There was great applause from the crowd! Later, I presented the cheque to the winner of the raffle after lunch and afternoon snacks.

I attended yet another Christmas Party at St. James's Palace on December 2nd. This time the Duchess of Kent received us. One of the Head Office executives acted as my escort.

On December 9th I was a guest of honour for the Carol Concert at the Guards' Chapel in Wellington Barracks. I was on the front row and was introduced to the large audience from the pulpit by an official and later by the chaplain. Afterwards, we proceeded to the Officers' Mess to attend the reception. Why did the VIPs make such a fuss of me?

Firstly the Duke and Duchess of Wellington, then very high-ranking officers of the Forces, then Lord and Lady Camoys, the Lord Chamberlain, Viscount Slim and Earl Haig – as well as a number of film personalities. Between 9.15 and 10pm, with a glass of champagne in my left hand, I was shaking hands with Lord "this" and Lady "that". Most of them wanted to know how or why I had lived so long. After standing for so long, I finally requested my chauffeur, but did not get back until midnight.

Pinewood Studios threw a party for us on December 10th and each resident received a gift for Christmas.

I intended to make this newsletter as short as possible so I have not included another 43 (forty-three) items! These all referred to visits by cameramen and reporters from various TV channels and local and national press – even from Scotland. There were also many visits from people whose grandfathers and relations served in the same regiment as myself. Very many were from people who had seen me on the TV, and it appears that I have been on television at least nine times. I actually had to turn down several would-be visitors and the requests to address pupils at schools, as I have done on two occasions.

Next week I am being escorted to the Waldorf Hotel in London to meet some screen celebrities; this will be televised, I understand. After all that, other activities will take place here. If past experience is anything to go by, they will be outstanding. Physically, I am in quite good shape, but unfortunately my eyesight is limiting my activities.

I have had another wonderful year and I am happy to state that I am receiving one hundred percent care in this lovely chateau. Had it not been so, I would not have been able to enjoy myself as I have done.

I have one regret. I shall not be seeing a fourth century, but I look forward to writing to you at this time in 2000. My best wishes for the festive season and "A GUID NEW YEAR TO YOU ALL".

Robert Burns December, 1999.

APPENDIX 6

The Secret

I've been asked one question so often:
"To what do you attribute your ripe old age?"

Firstly: sheer luck – for when I was three years young my Granny took me for a walk along the Crinan Canal. I must have been inquisitive for I fell into the water but was saved by the Lock-Keeper – so my parents told me in later years.

Secondly: I have to thank Lord Kitchener for his good advice which was – according to written instructions:

> *"Your duty cannot be done unless your health is good. So keep constantly on your guard against any excesses. In this new experience you may find many temptations both in Wine and Women. You must resist – entirely – both of these temptations and whilst treating all women with courtesy, YOU SHOULD AVOID ANY INTIMACY!*
>
> *Do your duty bravely For God Honour the King.*
>
> *LORD KITCHENER, 1914*

On reaching 100 years

Way back in Eighteen Ninety Five,
On the twelfth of the eleventh to be precise,
My Mother with her sparkling eyes,
Saw me kicking, full alive.

At Gourock on the River Clyde
'midst the beauty of the Firth,
My Father pranced with joy and pride,
To witness such a noble birth.

A Hundred I have reached today,
I've been looked after I must say,
At Glebelands House in Berkshire Royal,
By Matron, Staff – how they did toil.

Every day since my arrival,
I've been assured of my survival,
The Management - the Personnel,
Saw to it that I kept well.

The Residents and Convalescents
Me have rejuvenated,
Ever since I've been in residence,
I've been happy and elated.

What's next in store I can't foresee,
But a little older I shall be,
O'erlook the riches and the wealth,
I'll happier be with normal health.

Thank you all for coming here,
This anniversary to celebrate,
Let's sing that song both loud and clear,
Your friendship I'll not underrate.
   Robert Burns, 1995

Robert Burns (1895 – 2000)